# Grace Through Every Generation

## The Continuing Story
### of the
### Christian Reformed Church

FAITH
ALIVE®
Christian Resources

Grand Rapids, Michigan

# ACKNOWLEDGMENTS

The sesquicentennial committee is grateful for Rev. Hoezee's contribution to the observance of the 150th anniversary of the Christian Reformed Church in North America. This book is one of several initiatives that observes and expresses gratitude for God's *Grace Through Every Generation*.

Funding for this and other initiatives is contributed by generous donors through the CRC Foundation. To all of them we offer our thanks.

We're grateful to Richard Harms and the Heritage Hall archives at Calvin College, Grand Rapids, Michigan, for providing many of the photos that appear in this book.

We welcome your comments. Call us at 1-800-333-8300 or e-mail us at editors@faithaliveresources.org.

Library of Congress Cataloging-in-Publication Data
Hoezee, Scott, 1964-
  Grace through every generation: the continuing story of the Christian Reformed Church in North America/ Scott Hoezee.
   p. cm.
Includes bibliographical references.
ISBN 1-5955-294-3 (alk. paper)
1. Christian Reformed Church—History. I. Title.
BX6819.N7H64 2006
285.7'31—dc22

        2006013769


ISBN 1-59255-294-3

10 9 8 7 6 5 4 3 2 1

For David H. Engelhard
1941-2005

# CONTENTS

# PREFACE

As I completed this book during the week following Christmas in 2005, I sensed more keenly than ever something I knew would be true from the get-go: far more stories have been left out of this brief history than have been included. Yours may be one of them! And I'm sorry about that.

I wish there had been space to tell the story about what has happened these last fifty or so years across not just the full sweep of the Christian Reformed Church in North America but in many specific places too. I wish we could trace all the wonderful and blessed things that have happened through the work of World and Home Missions and through Christian Reformed World Relief Committee. I wish we had room to talk about what has changed at our institutes of higher learning: Calvin College, Calvin Theological Seminary, Dordt College, and Trinity Christian College in the United States; The King's

University College, Redeemer University College, and the Institute for Christian Studies in Canada. I wish we had time and space to discuss agency developments in the areas of chaplaincy, pastor-church relations, abuse prevention, and publishing, as well as the changes that have occurred over the years at the denominational mainstay *The Banner*. Some of these stories are told elsewhere, of course, but some are not.

Yet each of those stories (and ten thousand more besides) lies behind and beneath the stories that *are* told here. The broader sweeps of change and innovation that are told here would not have taken place the way they did were it not for the contributions, ideas, insights, and plain old hard work of untold (and largely unsung) people throughout the Christian Reformed Church these past 150 years (and certainly in the last fifty years on which this book will focus). Of course, merely acknowledging this will not get me off the hook with people who will want to know why such-and-such part of our shared story did not get told! But I do at least want to say up front that I recognize the disappointment some will feel in not having been mentioned.

Not long after taking on this assignment, I e-mailed a couple dozen church leaders and historians, soliciting their "Top Ten" list of key Christian Reformed events from 1957 to the present day. Thanks to their good responses, I was able to narrow down the focus of this book to what you see here. In some ways, parts of this book may read as much like a history of synod as of the wider denomination. But because ours is a polity (or church system) that brings local concerns up from the grass roots, what appeared on the various agendas for synod over the years did reflect in a real way the concerns of the rank-and-file members in the pews. Many of the key issues of the wider culture and of this most recent portion of world history—as well as many of the most dearly held and sometimes the most hotly contested issues within congregations during this last half century—did indeed become grist for the synodical mill. In any event, synod and what it said at key points in recent years is in part the place where I decided to sink various narrative fence posts in the corralling of our larger collective story.

I hope, in any event, that by perusing this book you will be able to gain a partial sense of where the CRCNA has been since 1957—where it has found cause to rejoice and sing and where it has found cause to lament and weep; where it has made changes seamlessly and easily and where it has changed through travail and tears. Because if there is one thing this story will make clear, it is that change has been the one constant in the last fifty years of our shared life together.

I have dedicated this book to my friend, teacher, and mentor, David Engelhard. I first met David when I was seven years old. At that time David was a freshly minted Ph.D. from Brandeis University and had just taken up a new teaching post at Calvin Theological Seminary. During that first year of teaching, David and his wife, Jeanne, were house-sitting for a year in the home of our backyard neighbors. Soon their eldest daughter Kris and I became fast friends and our two families enjoyed picnics and conversations together. Not long after this, my family moved and so did the Engelhards. We didn't see much of each other then. Fifteen years later when I enrolled at Calvin Theological Seminary in the M.Div. program, my old neighbor David Engelhard became my first seminary professor at "Hebrew Bootcamp"—a

David Engelhard

three-week summer intensive course that got all of us students accustomed to an alphabet that had to be read from right to left. David was a master instructor of language whose teaching I and others absorbed with delight and not a little awe.

David taught Hebrew and Old Testament for twenty-four years to hundreds of people who went on to become pastors in the CRCNA. In 1994 he surprised many colleagues and friends when he announced he was leaving the seminary to become General Secretary of the Christian Reformed denomination, succeeding Rev. Leonard Hofman.

For the next eleven years David thrived in his new position. He proved himself eminently capable of providing the organizational and detail-oriented knowledge necessary to a job that involved, among other things, culling vast quantities of information about the denomination as well as preparing the perennially unwieldy "Agenda for Synod." But David also traveled extensively and became the face of the CRC to a variety of church communions around the world. David introduced "fraternal delegates" to synod each year with an ardor and a sincerity that lent new warmth to the word "fraternal." And these representatives from denominations from around the world spoke with equal affection about David.

In late January 2004 I met with David in his office to discuss writing this sesquicentennial volume. The prospect of promoting a denomination-wide celebration of the CRCNA's 150th birthday was clearly a passion of David's, and he was deeply involved at most every level of planning. When I agreed to do this project, David thanked me warmly. He also told me, "You've got until the end of December 2005 to complete this manuscript—that's twenty-three months from now. I know it seems like a long time but it will go fast." Indeed it did. And as it turned out, that was—almost to the day—how much time David Engelhard had left on this earth. In February 2005 he was diagnosed with glioblastoma, a brain tumor known to be aggressive and incurable. David died ten months later on December 22, 2005.

At his funeral service family and friends testified that in his final months David was radiant with the hope of the gospel. His only comfort in life and in death became palpable to him in ways that inspired all who visited him. David's was a life worth celebrating in holy thanksgiving to the God who lent us this good servant, wonderful husband, and outstanding father and grandfather. "Grace through every generation" was a hallmark of David's life and family, and is his legacy to the church that he served so well as minister, theologian, scholar, teacher, and churchman. And so we give thanks to God for David's life and service as part of our celebration of the sesquicentennial of the CRCNA.

# INTRODUCTION:
# "THAT WAS THEN . . ."

My parents were married in 1959, just two years after the Christian Reformed Church celebrated its centennial anniversary in 1957. They were wed in a church in Holland, Michigan, about as close to the historical epicenter of the Reformed and Christian Reformed denominations as you can get. About the time I was starting to think about writing this history of the CRC's last fifty years, we celebrated a landmark wedding anniversary for my parents: their forty-fifth. As part of the celebration, we thought it might be fun to do a little "That Was Then" trivia contest focusing on key events and other cultural happenings of 1959. With a little help from the Internet, I was able to cobble together a small trove of 1959 facts and figures quite quickly. But when we held our trivia contest after the anniversary dinner, my parents were not able to answer many of the questions. The reason behind this may be quite revealing of the very historical shifts and changes that this book attempts to summarize.

When I asked my parents, for example, which movie had won the Academy Award for Best Picture in 1959, they had no idea—in the 1950s, Christian Reformed people did not go to the theater. It was still synodically forbidden, as a matter of fact (and would remain so until 1968), and so my parents had neither seen *Ben Hur* nor much cared that it had won an award. When I asked what the most popular song was for 1959, again they didn't know—most radios in their childhood homes were tuned to *The Back to God Hour*. Peter Eldersveld was a name they knew and a voice they loved to hear, but Bobby Darin singing "Mack the Knife" was not familiar. Finally, after a number of similar questions about the pop culture of 1959, my father said, "You have to understand: back then we stayed away from the wider culture and so we just didn't know much about it."

How things have indeed changed these past fifty years! Today the average twenty-year-old in the CRC not only attends movies, he or she may well have a growing collection of favorite DVDs. The youth of today, including those in the church, are outfitted with all the trappings of our technological age: laptops that connect to the Internet, portable CD players and iPods that can play thousands of hit songs, and cell phones with which to call their friends.

Preacher and writer Craig Barnes noted recently that the world is a vastly smaller, very different place for today's youth compared to just a generation or two ago. Barnes's daughter recently spent a semester studying in Europe. While there, she decided to spend a weekend in Budapest, where she withdrew some cash from an ATM, with which she bought some cappuccino at an Internet cafe, from which she sent an e-mail to her best friend, who was spending the semester studying in Brazil (Barnes, p. 48).

As Barnes notes, none of this seems extraordinary today, but compared to the way life was even as recently as 1957, it is clear that the world is an extraordinarily different place for us today. What we consider routine, our parents and grandparents would have considered so fantastically amazing as to count almost as a miracle. If you were to somehow transport forward in time a Christian Reformed person from the mid-1950s to the CRC of 2007, this time traveler might have a difficult time even recognizing what he or she would see. Upon closer inspection, this person would eventually find that the CRC beliefs, doctrines, and practices felt like home after all—but only after the shock had worn off from all that seemed so very different.

Of course, in its first hundred years, from 1857 to 1957, the CRC changed much, as did the world around it. But as this brief history will show, the past fifty years have introduced new dimensions to this denomination at a clip that outpaces most of the changes that came prior to this remarkable period of time.

Today the CRC is a richly diverse and varied body of believers. As the denomination turns 150 years of age, Christian Reformed worshipers can still find congregations where the pastor is a white man with a Dutch name, where worship is led by stately organ music and songs are sung from the *Psalter Hymnal,* and where liturgies are printed in predictable form week after week. On the other hand, there are also congregations where the pastor is a woman who hails originally from Korea, where worship is led by praise teams with steel guitars, and where everyone sings songs that are projected onto a screen. And in between these poles of traditional and contemporary, it's also possible to find just about every conceivable variation and combination of liturgical elements.

Although there was a measure of variety in the CRC even in 1957, it existed on a much narrower band width than is the case today. From British Columbia to New Jersey, from Florida to Toronto, most Christian Reformed churches in the 1950s still followed a pre-printed order of worship that varied almost not at all from week to week. Every Sunday morning and evening, the 211,000 souls who called the CRC home gathered in 495 churches across the United States and Canada. At that time, a Christian Reformed person on vacation—even far from home—could have wandered into just about any one of those hundreds of congregations without having to wonder in the least what to expect. The pastor, most likely a Calvin Theological Seminary graduate, would preach on the Heidelberg Catechism at one of the two Lord's Day services. The congregation would sing from the red *Psalter Hymnal*s found in the pew racks, and if there were any variation in the order of worship, it would be restricted to something no more dramatic than the placement of the offering.

However, vacationers away from home in 2007 have no reason to know what type of worship service to expect in a given CRC congregation. From the outside, it may even be difficult to be certain whether a church is Christian Reformed at all. You might have to read the small print on the

Worshipers from Golden Gate Christian Reformed Church, organized 1973

bulletin logo to find out that "Jubilee Community Church" is indeed a part of the CRC (and you might have to ask someone to be really sure).

But beyond the burgeoning variety of worship and the richness this variety has brought to the wider denomination, so much else has changed this last half-century, only a small portion of which can be chronicled in this book. The growth of the church in Canada is a remarkable story all by itself, as the number of Canadian members of the CRCNA grew from just over 37,000 in 1957 to nearly 60,000 in the early twenty-first century—an increase of nearly 40 percent (mostly as a result of immigration from the Netherlands) over a period of time in which the entire denomination increased just 23 percent over its 1957 membership total.

The explosion of various other ethnic groups also signifies changes in the CRC. At mid-century, many Christian Reformed people could still remember the days when in a given city you could choose whether to attend the Dutch-speaking church or the one that had finally made the switch to English. Today services conducted in Dutch are at best a once-a-year event to commemorate the past, whereas services in Korean, Spanish, and Chinese are weekly occurrences. In fact, the denomination now has entire classes (or groups of churches) comprised solely of various ethnic groups.

Theologically, the CRC has also addressed issues and made changes in its official polity as a result of rich scholarship that has challenged and educated Christians far beyond the borders of the denomination itself.

So although this volume is a celebration of the CRCNA's sesquicentennial, the past fifty of this denomination's 150 years will occupy us the most. A good deal of what the CRC is in 2007 comes as much from the last half-century as it does from all the years that formed the church in the years prior to 1957. And much of what may happen as we move forward as a denomination may also prove to have stemmed from changes that occurred in the recent past.

But whether we look back at periods of relative calm and stability in the history of the CRC or examine times of great change and controversy, the truth of "grace through every generation" always shines through. The CRCNA is not the largest segment of our Lord's history-long and worldwide church, nor is it more important or vital than any other part of the body of Christ. But the Lord whose "eye is on the sparrow" takes providential note and care of all his people, wherever they worship and whenever they come together to work for the kingdom's advance. Jesus Christ is the Lord of the church. His grace extends through every generation of this story. The history of any church is always first and last about the God whose grace is more than sufficient to stick with us through the peaks and valleys of every story we can tell about church life.

It is the story of this God and of God's grace that we want to tell to all generations yet to come.

*ဢ* *Chapter One* *Ꮳ*

# THE FIRST HUNDRED YEARS:
# A LOOK BACK

For many years I had the opportunity to teach my congregation's high school catechism class. In truth, we didn't always study the Heidelberg Catechism but made forays into the Belgic Confession, the ecumenical creeds, and other doctrinal summaries of the faith. But no matter what the specific topic of study was in any given year, at some point I would give a brief review of the history of the Christian Reformed Church. To set the wider historical stage, we also reviewed the larger Protestant Reformation from which the CRCNA ultimately derived. It was always interesting to watch students' reactions when I told them that for basically half of all the years the Christian church on earth has existed, it formed essentially one giant worldwide denomination known as the Catholic Church and was headed by the pope in Rome.

To high schoolers born in the late twentieth century, that kind of global unity seems nearly unimaginable. For instance, in 2004 the Grand Rapids,

Michigan, Yellow Pages listed 100 different denominations. Among those were twelve variations on Baptist denominations, four discrete denominations that called themselves Reformed, four different varieties of Lutherans, and another four variations on being Presbyterian.

As I used to tell my students, one of the finest features of the Protestant Reformation was not only a return to the Bible as the final authority but also getting Scripture into the hands of ordinary people, not just clergy. One of the first things Martin Luther did after his break with the Catholic Church was to translate the Bible into German so that every literate person could read it. Until then, the Bible had been in Latin or in Greek, languages most ordinary Christians could not read (if they could read anything at all). Prior to the invention of the printing press in the fifteenth century, there were no books for ordinary people to own anyway. But the ability to crank out lots of books made possible by the printing press, together with Luther's translation of the Bible into the language of the people, suddenly made real what had been unthinkable: ordinary Christians could have their own personal copy of the Bible. As a result, they no longer needed to rely on priests to tell them what the Bible said. They could be their own biblical interpreter. Of course, the community of faith still needed to agree on matters collectively in reliance on the Holy Spirit. But now each person (not just the clergy) could bring his or her thoughts about the Bible into that wider discussion.

Getting the Bible into the hands of Christian lay people was a wonderful gift. But along with the gift came an unintended consequence. Not surprisingly, having lots of people reading the same text led to lots of different opinions on that text! And within a generation of Luther and Calvin, the Protestant wing of the church had splintered into multiple factions that eventually turned into different denominations, each led by a particular school of biblical and theological interpretation.

Sometimes I would draw a diagram for my high school class: from the time of Christ forward, the history of the church formed one long continuous line, with a single breakaway line at the year 1056, right up until the mid-1500s. From there, the Roman Catholic line continues pretty much unbroken to this day. But the Protestant line ends up looking like the pattern you see on a car windshield that's been cracked with a big rock: spider web-like tendrils snaking off in all directions.

The genius of the Reformation was a return to the Bible. Yet in one of history's sharper ironies, that unified return to Scripture resulted in the most profound disunity the church has ever known. That's why my students could barely wrap their minds around that long period of history when denominational diversity did not exist. The idea of a unified church of Jesus Christ on earth was as quaint to their young minds as the vinyl LPs their parents used to play on a turntable. In our age of ever-growing denominational diversity, looking back on a unified church is like peering into a world none of us has ever known firsthand.

The history of the past five hundred years bears unhappy witness to the fact that one church schism tends to beget others. And even where actual schism does not occur, the specter of potential future breaches of fellowship looms over every important discussion churches have. The CRC is certainly no exception. After all, there's no escaping the fact that it grew out of several nineteenth-century church splits both in the Netherlands and in the United States. Throughout its history, the CRCNA has tried, successfully for the most part, to hold together in unity a group of Reformed Christians who, although sharing a common heritage and biblical-theological foundation, came to the denomination through several different historical paths, each sufficiently different from the others to generate some tension. At its best, this has been a creative tension that has sparked fine scholarship and biblical interpretation. At its worst, however, this tension has grown to the breaking point, which is why, in part, the denomination produced a couple of further fractures in the twentieth century.

## Nineteenth Century Roots

Because this sesquicentennial volume focuses on the CRCNA's most recent half-century, this chapter is a quick review of the first hundred years, a period of denominational history that has been well-documented in many other places, including James Schaap's delightful book *Our Family Album: The Unfinished Story of the Christian Reformed Church* (1998). As already indicated, to tell the full story of the Christian Reformed Church one could go all the way back to the Reformation and then trace the subsequent offshoots throughout Europe, especially in the Netherlands. Instead, we will turn back the clock to 1834 to set the stage for the most immediate backdrop to the formation of the CRC.

By the early 1800s, the Reformed church in the Netherlands had essentially become the state church. But, as often happens when a church body becomes large and official, it sometimes begins to assume a profile that is perceived to be very different from the olden days. In this case, church leaders began to suspect that the church had become not only official but a bit officious. Doctrines were the stuff of state policy as much as, if not more than, the stuff of personal devotion.

But there were structural issues that proved nettlesome as well. For instance, some in the Dutch church, known for its adherence to singing only settings of the Psalms, were highly displeased when in 1816 the government decreed that all churches would henceforth be required to add hymns to their weekly worship services. This did not sit well with some church leaders for a couple of reasons. First, the top-down, authoritarian nature of the decision was at odds with the traditional Reformed way of decision-making, in which congregations were supposed to participate in making major decisions. But it also seemed to be a step in the wrong direction in a spiritual sense: the old heritage was being left behind in favor of a new future that many were not willing to embrace.

Psalmbook used in the Dutch Reformed Church and also by the early CRC and RCA in North America

During this same period, a spiritual revival was sweeping across Europe. This return to piety and devoutness—a movement that many trace back to Geneva (the old stomping grounds of John Calvin himself)—eventually reached the Netherlands in the form of a movement called the *Reveil*, which meant to "wake up." Led by poet and historian Willem Bilderdijk (1756-1831), this return to spiritual devoutness soon encompassed a number of Reformed pastors who, already dissatisfied with the direction taken by the state church, discovered in the *Reveil* the final nudge they needed to push for an all-out reformation of the Dutch church. The drive for this ecclesiastical makeover had both an urban and a rural component, and the differences between the two (and how they ultimately combined within the CRC many years later) form a key part of what eventually coalesced in the character of the denomination.

When efforts to work with the state church proved unsuccessful, some *Reveil*-influenced pastors acted decisively. In 1834 the secession that became known as the *Afscheiding* took place when Rev. Hendrik de Cock and his Ulrum congregation formally decided to break away from the state church. Others soon followed, including Hendrik

Pieter Scholte, the man who would later found the Dutch colony in Pella, Iowa, and Albertus C. Van Raalte, the founder of Holland, Michigan, who at the time of the *Afscheiding* had just graduated from seminary. Van Raalte, who was ordained in 1836, would be one of many immigrants who would later help to transplant the newly formed church to a faraway place called America.

However, tracing back the precise origin of the CRCNA does not end with the 1834 secession. The next part of the story takes place in the United States. By the time of the *Afscheiding*, there were already many Dutch immigrants living in North America, especially concentrated in New York and New Jersey. These immigrants had forged an American version of the church known then as the Dutch Reformed Church (later called the Reformed Church in America). By the mid-1800s the Dutch Reformed Church was firmly established with approximately 274 congregations totaling nearly 33,000 members. What's more, these immi-

Hendrik de Cock, leader of the secession known as the *Afscheiding*

grants had even managed to establish two schools: Rutgers College and New Brunswick Theological Seminary (Beets, p. 44). So by the time the *Reveil*-influenced pastors and parishioners of the 1834 secession began coming to the United States in the mid-1800s, an established Reformed presence in the New World was eager to enfold them.

By the mid- to late-1840s, newly formed colonies had been established in Wisconsin, Illinois, Michigan, and Iowa. Despite all the rigors and perils that were part and parcel of the immigrant experience (and despite ravaging diseases that at times threatened to decimate the newly formed colonies), Van Raalte's colony in Holland, Michigan, and Scholte's in Pella, Iowa, were large enough to catch the eye of the Reformed Church leadership. The East Coast-based denomination dispatched representatives to the Midwest to invite these Dutch brothers and sisters into an ecclesiastical partnership. In

Albertus C. Van Raalte

Hendrik Pieter Scholte

the spring of 1849, Rev. Isaac Wyckoff of the Reformed Church paid a visit to Classis Holland, which at that time consisted of Van Raalte's own congregation in Holland, Michigan, as well as neighboring congregations in Zeeland, Vriesland, and Graafschap. At a meeting the previous September, these congregations had briefly considered making a formal overture to become part of the Reformed Church in America but had delayed action, citing "the pressure of local business and the difficulties connected with a new settlement" (Schaap, p. 135). In short, they were barely hanging on and had scant energy to consider anything as ambitious as merging with a wider denomination.

Nonetheless, Rev. Wyckoff's arrival in 1849 set into motion a series of events that eventually made Classis Holland part of the larger Reformed presence in the United States. By then the number of Reformed congregations in West Michigan totaled seven. But there was some confusion and controversy as to how this came about. Wyckoff returned home reporting these congregations as being on board. The colonists were uncertain as to how official this all was. Not until 1850, following Van Raalte's attendance of the Reformed Church synod in Schenectady, New York, was the union plainly official. But seeds of doubt concerning the wisdom of this union had already been sown. A few years later Van Raalte would experience the bitter fruit that came once those seeds sprouted and grew.

By the 1850s, some of the Dutch Reformed believers in West Michigan began to detect in the American version of the Reformed Church some of the same characteristics that had driven them out of the Dutch state church in 1834 to begin with. Already in 1849, when Wyckoff visited Classis Holland, he sensed some unease toward being part of yet another larger church body. These congregations feared losing control over key decisions in a situation similar to what had happened in the old country. As part of his effort both to assure and to woo these immigrants, Wyckoff said they would be under no obligation to remain in the American Reformed denomination should they someday want to leave; they would always be free "to bid us a fraternal adieu and be by themselves again" (Beets, p. 57). As Henry Beets stated, this was "a typically American way of surmounting the obstacle encountered, although not according to Reformed principles of church government . . . [But] the Michigan Dutchmen accepted the reservation at face value and stored it in their memory."

Indeed they did. What's more, as some Michigan colonies learned more and more about the Reformed Church in the East, they liked it less and less. It was the 1834 *Afscheiding* all over again, as people began to lodge formal complaints about departures from the traditional Church Order, including singing hymns instead of psalms only, the practice of private baptisms and open communion, and toleration of Free Masons lodge members within Reformed congregations. By the April 8, 1857, meeting of the Reformed Church Classis of Holland, four congregations had sent notices of withdrawal.

But these changes did not come out of the blue. For several years many West Michigan leaders, including Rev. Koenraad Van Den Bosch of Noordelos and church elder Gijsbert Haan from nearby Grand Rapids, had been agitating for change and accusing even Van Raalte of being too lax on matters of doctrine and the purity of the church. Van Den Bosch and his Noordelos congregation believed that Van Raalte's 1850 union with the Reformed Church in America had placed all of them right back into the same situation that had existed in the Netherlands before 1834. If the first *Afscheiding* had been the right thing to do, it seemed their present course was obvious: they needed to get out of this American version of the old state church. By April 29, 1857, a formal organizational meeting was attended by five West Michigan congregations. Together they formed a new classis. Ultimately, this new entity

Koenraad Van Den Bosch

Gijsbert Haan

would become known as the Christian Reformed Church in North America.

In subsequent years, other congregations followed Van Den Bosch's lead and joined the new denomination, which called itself initially the *Hollandsche Gereformeerde Kerk* (the Dutch Reformed Church) and then later the *Ware Hollandsche Gereformeerde Kerk* (the True Dutch Reformed Church). Not until 1880 did the group adopt a version of the name "Christian Reformed Church." For the first twenty or so years of its life, the early CRC existed as what James Schaap calls "an orphan" off by itself in a still-strange New World. Records of those early years bear witness to the grace of God that the fledgling group managed to survive at all. There is evidence of a series of disagreements and uncertainties as well as no small amount of infighting. As noted earlier, the positive dimension of people who are fiercely committed to purity and truth is that their passion can be second to none. But this same tendency to get things exactly right can also become a club with which to bludgeon those who disagree. As Schaap notes, our denomination's earliest classis meetings "were riddled with lists of charges and countercharges of heresy as long as your arm" (Schaap, p. 169).

Throughout the 1860s new churches were formed as part of the CRC in Zeeland, Michigan, in what is now South Holland, Illinois, and even as far away from the West Michigan epicenter as New Jersey, Ohio, Iowa, and Indiana. In 1865 the first meeting of what would later be known as synod took place in Graafschap, Michigan. On February 14, 1868, the eleven-year-old denomination published its first in-house periodical, *De Wachter.*

The first editor of *De Wachter* was a West Michigan powerhouse whose efforts on multiple fronts helped the CRC thrive and move forward: Rev. D. J. Van der Werp. In addition to being the pastor of the Graafschap congregation and founding editor of the denomination's first magazine, Van der Werp also began training students in theology in order to help them become future pastors in the denomination. Van der Werp continued this work until age and declining health forced him to stop, but his vision of an educated clergy planted the seed for what would eventually become Calvin Theological Seminary and later also Calvin College.

Graafschap CRC, organized 1847

Originally called the Theological School of the Christian Reformed Church, this new institute of learning got its formal beginning on March 15, 1876 (a date subsequently known to all Calvin Seminary students as *Dies Natalis,* the "day of birth" for the CRC's official seminary). On that date, Rev. Gerrit E. Boer (1832-1904), who had just become the school's full-time professor, delivered a convocation address on "The Training of Future Ministers of the Gospel." In the school year that followed, the seven-member student body received from Boer an education that ran the gamut from language studies in Latin, Greek, and Hebrew to philosophical disciplines, rhetoric, and, of course, the theological disciplines in systematic theology, church history, exegesis, and practical theology. An impressive display indeed for this one-man faculty! Boer began what would become a hallmark of the CRC: a tradition of excellent liberal arts education conducted under rigorous academic standards and

Students at Calvin Theological Seminary, 1877

aimed always at engaging God's world. A century after Boer's pioneering work, Calvin College and Calvin Theological Seminary are known nationwide as being among the finest institutions of higher education anywhere. Many Calvin graduates and former professors have gone on to make their mark in the annals of academia, putting the CRC on the map as much for its excellence in scholarship as anything else.

By the late 1870s, the CRC had grown sufficiently to warrant the organization of new classes in Illinois (1868), Iowa (1877), and on the East Coast (Hudson, 1878). Meanwhile, back in the Netherlands, another secession was brewing—one that would ultimately have a direct and long-lasting effect on the CRCNA. Nearly fifty years after the *Afscheiding* from the Dutch state church, another breakaway group was forming, led by Abraham Kuyper, one of the most remarkable figures in the history of the Dutch Reformed movement. Kuyper (1837-1920) was a man of keen intellect, deep insight, and wide-ranging interests. He was committed to engaging with society and the wider world and did so as prime minister of the Netherlands from 1901-1905.

But Kuyper was also a preacher who had grown up in and worked as a pastor for the same state church that the 1834 seceders had left. Kuyper was born three years after the *Afscheiding* to parents who, although sympathetic to the cause of the seceders, never wanted to leave their home church. About the time the CRC was being founded across the ocean in Holland, Michigan, Kuyper graduated from the University of Leiden and entered the ministry. As historian James Bratt and others have noted, Kuyper was an unlikely figure to become associated with the heirs of the *Afscheiding*. Kuyper's mind embraced tensions and possessed a worldview that was more urbane and tinged with modernism than was typical of the more pietistic traditionalists who founded the CRC in 1857. But because Kuyper led a movement out of the same mother church as the *Afscheiding* group, when many of Kuyper's followers came to the United States, as in the large wave of Dutch immigration that took place between 1870-1920, they found in the CRC enough commonality of mind, thought, and heritage that they joined the denomination gladly.

Abraham Kuyper

The movement Kuyper founded became known as the *Doleantie*, which meant "the grieving church." By 1883, Kuyper had gained a reputation as a powerful preacher. His ideas resonated with many who, like Kuyper, began to suspect more and more that the state church, known as the *Hervormde Kerk*, was drifting both doctrinally and in official church practice. Like his parents, Kuyper wanted to reform the church from within. But when, in 1883, the church formally rejected the requirement for officebearers to conform with the confessions of the Reformed faith (known to this day within the CRC as signing the "form of subscription"), it became clear to Kuyper and his followers that they could no longer remain. Just in case the *Doleantie* folks were unsure about the need to secede, the state church settled the matter for them by deposing those pastors who continued to lament this step back from the confessions. Abraham Kuyper was among the deposed.

The followers of the *Doleantie* formally organized themselves in 1892 into the *Christelijk Gereformeerde Kerk*, which means "Christian Reformed Church" (the name shows why Kuyper's followers were attracted to the North American denomination with that same moniker once many of them immigrated around the turn of the century). In 1894 churches in the United States were permitted to use the name "Christian Reformed Church" (initially they had been called the Dutch Reformed Church and then later the True Dutch Reformed Church); the full adoption of the name Christian Reformed Church came in 1904.

The influx of the *Doleantie* forever changed the complexion of the denomination. In his brilliant history *Dutch Calvinism in Modern America,* Calvin College history professor James Bratt highlighted the differences by noting that the CRC, at least since 1900, has always been a mixture of mentalities, any one of which can ultimately be traced back to either the *Afscheiding* or to the *Doleantie.* What the mindset of the *Afscheiding* brought to the CRC was a strong strain of pietism and confessionalism that tended to be rather defensive in its theology and frankly suspicious of whether, or to what extent, the wider culture could or should be engaged. For its part, the *Doleantie* tended to be more outgoing and optimistic, willing to engage the world and seeing great potential for good to come out of a constructive theology that was willing to push at the margins for new ideas and strategies.

As Bratt notes, even within these two broadly defined schools of thought there were further subsets. In general, however, the CRCNA continues to this day to live with some of these historical tensions. Even contemporary debates on the floor of synod contain echoes of this tension. Bratt claims that the more *Afscheiding*-influenced wing, which he calls the "Confessionalists," advocate strongly for tradition, for a tightly defined form of what constitutes orthodoxy, and so tend to speak against approaches to Scripture that seem novel or that could produce results that would be at potential variance with the thoughts expressed in the Heidelberg Catechism and other such Reformed documents. On the other hand, the "Doleantie" descendants Bratt calls "Positive Calvinists" often seem willing to test the ideas of the past against more up-to-date hermeneutics and theological reflection, displaying a willingness not only to engage the wider society but even to recognize that sometimes the insights of the surrounding world can help Christian people refine their thinking and theology.

As we will see in coming chapters, even some of the great issues that occupied the CRCNA in the last half century bear witness to the fact that there is no escaping history.

## The New Century

At the same time these broader influences on the make-up of the young denomination were taking place, the CRC initiated a number of endeavors that, over time, greatly increased its influence in North America, even as the church itself grew in numbers because of the new programs. By 1900 the CRC encompassed a total of nearly 54,000 members belonging to 144 congregations. Although still concentrated largely in the Midwest, the Christian Reformed presence extended literally from coast to coast and many places in between. The East Coast had long been a CRC stronghold and was strengthened in 1890 with the formation of Classis Hackensack, the second East Coast classis in the denomination. In 1900 the CRC went far west with the founding of a Christian Reformed congregation in Lynden, Washington. Additional congregations were founded in the Dakotas, in Kansas, and throughout Minnesota.

In 1896 the CRC began also a new venture in the area of domestic or home missions. As noted earlier, the first quarter-century of the CRC's existence was a tenuous, often difficult, era. The fledgling denomination had all it could do to survive and to establish the structures that would be needed to forge ahead. But by the last part of the nineteenth century, many became concerned that this inward focus, although perhaps necessary initially, had become an abiding characteristic in ways that made it difficult for the CRC to fulfill the Great Commission of spreading the gospel to all the world. Eventually those voices got the attention of the synod, and the denomination founded what it called (indelicate though this sounds to our twenty-first century ears) "The Board of Heathen Missions."

In the book *Flourishing in the Land,* Christopher Meehan and I chronicled the CRC's first 100 years of domestic mission activity in North America. The story began in the Old West on an October day in 1896 when Andrew Vander Wagen and Herman Fryling and their wives arrived in Gallup, New Mexico, to begin the CRC's first-ever attempt at missions among the Navajo people. The work began modestly among the Navajo people located near Fort Defiance. A year later the Vander Wagens had left that work to the Frylings and had shifted their efforts to the Zuni pueblo south of the area around Gallup. In coming years the mission effort spread out to the surrounding areas, the most significant of which became known eventually as Rehoboth.

Around the turn of the century it was a common practice of both the United States government and of church mission agencies to establish Indian

Hull (North Dakota) CRC, organized 1887

boarding schools. Although painful to recount, the unhappy historical fact is that Native Americans were generally regarded as "savages." For a long time it was believed that the only way to turn them into useful, productive members of American society was to whisk children out of their homes and place them in schools that would stamp out (and sometimes beat out) all vestiges of Indian culture, replacing it with white ways of thinking and behaving. In 1903 the CRC used this boarding school model when it established its own mission at Rehoboth, just outside of Gallup. Although its earliest days bore too much resemblance to the many institutions that vandalized Native American culture, over the years the school developed into an excellent place of learning that continues in the twenty-first century. What's more, those initial efforts of the Vander Wagens and the Frylings flourished to the point that Classis Red Mesa was established in 1982. Today Red Mesa encompasses seventeen congregations with just over 2,000 members throughout New Mexico and Arizona.

But it was not only in the American Southwest that the CRC grew and expanded through its mission efforts. World Wars I and II forced the at-times sheltered members of the CRC out into a wider world, even as the GI Bill after World War II altered the American (and Christian Reformed) landscape as millions of people were able to take advantage of the possibility of higher education. These wars also led to the founding of chaplaincy ministries in the CRC. Although chaplaincy began in the military in World War I, the ministry of Christian Reformed pastors serving as chaplains extended to include university campuses, hospitals, retirement communities, prisons, and hospice programs.

In 1939 the CRC's efforts to have a presence on the airwaves culminated with the inaugural broadcast of *The Back to God Hour.* The program opened with a prayer by Rev. Henry Schultze asking God to enable

Rehoboth mission school, 1908

the new radio show "to move men everywhere to a renewed consciousness of the great glory of our God" (Hoezee and Meehan, p. 79). Carried on Chicago station WJJD, that December 17 broadcast began a tradition of excellence in radio and, later, television.

The early years of *The Back to God Hour* featured a variety of on-air speakers and ministers, but by 1947 one name alone stood out as the voice of the CRC on the radio— Peter Eldersveld. For the next eighteen years until his sudden death from a heart attack in 1965, Eldersveld crafted a radio show that was cherished by members of the CRC but also succeeded in reaching out to a vast audience with the gospel. Eldersveld's unexpected death created a shock wave that swept over the entire denomination.

By God's grace and providence, Eldersveld's able successor was already in the wings.

United States Army Chaplain InSoon Gho

Joel Nederhood had been working with Eldersveld for some time and was seen as the natural choice to take over the show. Nederhood remained for the next thirty years. During that time, nearly twice as long as Eldersveld's tenure, Nederhood continued the Back to God Hour's tradition of stalwart Reformed preaching aimed at bringing the good news to the world. Nederhood also oversaw an expansion of the foreign language broadcasts that had begun in Eldersveld's day and helped the ministry transition into television during the late 1970s.

Other portions of the CRC's work on the domestic front will be told in subsequent chapters of this book, including the growth of the denomination in Canada as well as the success of many urban mission efforts that have, in part, contributed to the CRC's growing ethnic diversity.

Peter Eldersveld, radio minister for *The Back to God Hour*

Meanwhile, the denomination also initiated foreign missions. By 1920 CRC member Johanna Veenstra was laboring in the Sudan (although not as an official missionary of the CRC). Synod 1920 declared that similar mission efforts would be made in China, an effort that was initially spearheaded by people whose names have become nearly synonymous with Christian Reformed missions in the early days: Lee Huizinga, Wilhelmina Kalsbeek, and A. H. Smit. Along with their families, and often through great hardship, these people began a kind of foreign mission work that would grow and expand, especially in the second half of the century. For her part, Johanna Veenstra moved her work from the Sudan to Nigeria. And although there may have been some initial hesitancy in 1930 when she requested financial support from the denomination, and despite the fact that she died in 1933, by mid-century it was clear that the work Veenstra had begun in Nigeria simply had to be continued. Nigeria went on to become a fruitful field for Christian Reformed mission work and is now home to many CRC-related congregations with nearly 200,000 worshipers each Sunday.

During the past half-century, Christian Reformed World Missions has witnessed a steady expansion of its work in every corner of the world. Although the rise of communism after 1949 made missionary work in many places (including China) difficult, if not impossible, other fields continued to open up. Central America, South America, Asia, and Africa became the targets of concerted efforts to bring the gospel in both word and deed.

The "deed" portion of that work was magnified immensely after 1960 with the formal establishment of a diaconal service agency called Christian Reformed World Relief Committee. CRWRC went on to become an agency able to respond quickly to natural disasters such as hurricanes and earthquakes as well as to sponsor longer-term programs designed to enable people to provide for themselves and their communities. CRWRC also tried to increase people's health in disease-prone areas of the world by digging wells to provide clean drinking water and by bringing medicines and health care.

Johanna Veenstra, missionary

Today the Christian Reformed presence on earth can be truly described as global. In addition to ministries of all kinds throughout the United States and Canada, World Missions and CRWRC have established a presence in the Ivory Coast, Gambia, Guinea, Mali, Nigeria, Kenya, Malawi, Rwanda, South Africa, Tanzania, Uganda, Zambia, Bangladesh, Cambodia, China, Taiwan, Japan, Guam, Laos, Indonesia, Thailand, the Philippines, France, Hungary, Russia, the Netherlands, Haiti, the Dominican Republic, Belize, Costa Rica, El Salvador, Honduras, Nicaragua, Ecuador, Guatemala, and Mexico. Clearly those in the late nineteenth century who knew that the CRC could not remain inwardly focused can be credited with not only helping the denomination be faithful to the Great Commission but also with helping the CRC to flourish and become a key part of the larger North American and the global church scene.

In 1907 the CRC turned fifty. On its golden anniversary, the denomination could look back gratefully at how far it had come. With a total membership of around 63,000 members in 165 congregations, the CRC was still much smaller than the Reformed Church in America, which numbered 154,000

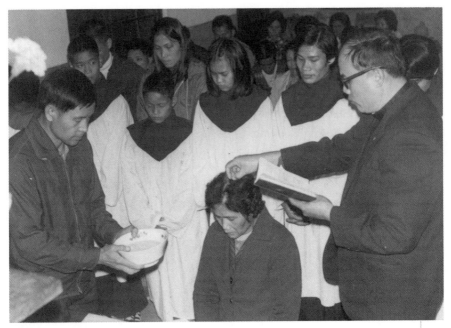

Baptism in China

souls nationwide. But the CRC was about to begin one of its strongest periods of growth ever, more than tripling its membership and nearly tripling its
total number of congregations by 1957. Of course, this second fifty-year period of CRC history was also at times tumultuous. Along with the rest of the
world, Christian Reformed members endured the terrible shocks of two
world wars, a severe economic depression, news of the Holocaust, and, by
mid-century, looming fears of nuclear annihilation. As often happens, the
stress caused by times of global crisis sometimes fosters stress in other areas.
Tense times tend to make people tense about everything.

Some of that stress may account for the CRC's struggles in the first half of
the twentieth century, but there were also internal sources of anxiety. As
noted earlier, the influx of members associated with Kuyper's *Doleantie*
secession in the Netherlands introduced new members to the CRC who,
although speaking basically the same Reformed language as the descendants of the *Afscheiding*, spoke that mother tongue with a rather different
theological accent. In addition to this potential source of disagreement on
some of the finer points of theology, the CRC was finally an immigrant
denomination. As such, it faced the challenges that all immigrant groups
eventually encounter. Over time, the older generation, who still spoke Dutch

and who had come directly from the Netherlands, gave way to the next generation, who were born in America and preferred to speak English.

The first congregation I served was Second CRC in Fremont, Michigan. Second CRC, like many congregations around the denomination, traces its roots back to 1914. By that time, Fremont already had two Christian Reformed congregations in close proximity, one in the heart of Fremont and the other in neighboring Reeman. So why was it necessary to establish yet another congregation? The issue in Fremont and in many places in the early twentieth century was the language used in worship. Second CRC in Fremont was founded by those who wanted to worship in English instead of Dutch. Those who opposed this switch to the language of the land appealed to far more than a traditionalism of the "we never did it that way before" variety. During those years of transition and struggle from one language to the other, serious articles were written in *De Wachter* and *The Banner* alleging that it might not even be possible to adhere to Reformed theology in a language other than Dutch. Something might get lost (or worse, corrupted) in translation. To be Reformed was to speak Dutch!

Over time, of course, this controversy faded as fewer and fewer Christian Reformed members spoke Dutch even in their homes, much less at church. But other cultural pressures also came to bear on the denomination, some of which were expressed in theological pronouncements. The third decade of the twentieth century was known as "The Roaring 20s" in the secular world. The CRC roared in those years too—but not in the exuberant manner of the wider society. Instead the denomination was consumed with controversy and rife with attempts to hold at bay the influence of the world.

The 1920s began with controversy when Professor Ralph Janssen, who taught Old Testament at Calvin Theological Seminary, was accused of teaching his students un-Reformed views of Scripture. Critics feared a creeping form of incipient liberalism that was being imported to North America from the liberal citadels of European—especially German—universities. Janssen, they claimed, was diminishing the sacred character of God's holy Word by taking a rationalistic approach to some of the miracles in the Old Testament (suggesting, for instance, that God could have worked through natural phenomena in nature). Janssen was also accused of undercutting the inspired nature of the Bible by promoting the idea that the Bible had resulted from a long and complicated process of editing and piecing together by many writers and editors across many centuries of time. Janssen's seminary colleagues tried twice (and failed twice) to make the seminary board take action. When these professors felt that Synod 1920 had failed to go far enough in reprimanding Janssen, they communicated their concerns to the wider denomination through articles and brochures. This stirred things up sufficiently so that by 1921 the board gave Janssen a year-long "vacation" from teaching. Janssen used his free time to defend himself and attack his most vociferous

Ralph Janssen

opponents, chiefly colleagues Foppe Ten Hoor, and also Rev. Herman Hoeksema, who had been using his regular column in *The Banner* to pillory Janssen's teachings. When Janssen refused to appear before the delegates to defend himself in person, the synod moved to depose him on the grounds of insubordination and heresy.

It was a victory for Janssen's critics, including Herman Hoeksema. But, as James Bratt notes, "Hoeksema would soon learn that the sword of hatred cut more ways than one" (Bratt, p. 110). Within just a few years' time, Hoeksema would find himself on the losing end of a synodical battle that forced him to leave the CRC. If the Janssen case was a CRC battle to keep European liberalism at bay, the Hoeksema matter was more in-house, as it caused the CRC to grapple with common grace, one of the teachings imported by Abraham Kuyper's followers. As much as anything, common grace encapsulated the outgoing and optimistic side of the Positive Calvinists—an optimism that grew well in the soil of the optimistic American spirit of the 1920s. But some folks from the Confessionalist side of the Reformed tradition had always been suspicious of this belief. Dealing with common grace was, in a sense, an accident waiting to happen.

And in the mid-1920s it did. Without describing the ins and outs of this controversy, we can summarize by reporting what synod said. In the end, synod affirmed that there is such a thing as common grace, which is not the same thing as saving grace in Christ but is a divine gift that is present even in the lives of unbelievers. Through common grace God manifests a certain favor toward all creatures by which God both restrains sin from being as bad as it could be in individuals and in whole societies, and God nurtures good gifts in people—gifts that enable also non-Christians to do civic good, produce excellence in the arts, and generally contribute to goodness in all of life.

But some in the CRC dissented from these ideas, and Herman Hoeksema became their chief spokesman. Hoeksema and others ardently believed that the very word "grace" had to be restricted to God's saving work through Christ Jesus. The "total depravity" of unregenerate reprobates was total indeed: they were incapable of producing works that could be considered "good" in any sense worth talking about.

Herman Hoeksema

More was at stake here than some fine point of theological reflection. Those opposed to the concept shared a palpable fear that embracing common grace would erode the differences between the church and American culture, possibly opening up the floodgates through which an ugly tide of worldliness would flow. They feared that if the CRC became still more Americanized by promoting common grace, it risked losing all that made the Reformed heritage so dear to their hearts. With so much at stake, the battle became fierce. Although Synod 1924 weighed in on the side of promoting common grace, they surrounded this affirmation with ringing warnings against modernism and worldliness. It urged all Christian Reformed congregations "to fight tooth and nail" to maintain the antithesis, the abiding distinction, between society and the church (quoted in Bratt, p. 115).

If this kind of world-shunning sentiment was intended to soften the blow of synod's wider endorsement of common grace, it did not succeed. Hoeksema railed all the more against synod's decision in published materials and from his pulpit at Eastern Avenue CRC in Grand Rapids. The ensuing controversy eventually led to discipline procedures against Hoeksema and his ouster from the denomination. Those who followed him out of the CRC formed the Protestant Reformed churches.

Delegates at Synod 1924

A split in the church is always the unhappiest possible outcome in any disagreement among Christians. This particular split remains painful for many, and not infrequently there are pleas to investigate healing the rift. But, as is often the case, after many years of being apart, subsequent developments tend to widen the differences between two groups to the point where what may have been a fairly small gap starts to look more like a chasm.

For its part, synod continued to affirm its desire to build a barrier between the church and the world. In a speakeasy society where flappers danced the Charleston and where the nickelodeon was becoming all the rage, Synod 1928 took a stand against "worldly amusements," outlawing for the CRC faithful the practices of gambling, dancing, and theater attendance. Again to quote Bratt's assessment, the 1920s ended with the CRC erecting a kind of religious fortress. Common grace had been upheld, which was a kind of victory for the more outgoing wing of the Reformed tradition. But the rest of the decade witnessed a firm holding of the traditional line. Inside the ecclesiastical fortress that the CRC had built for itself, church members would huddle together to endure the terrible years that were about to come crashing down upon the world.

By the time the world emerged from the rigors and horrors of the 1930s and 40s, the CRC had managed nearly two decades of relative calm. The denomination added seventy-eight new congregations and 40,000 members. While the world had been in turmoil, the church had been relatively tranquil. But that was about to change in the 1950s. Perhaps it is no coincidence that the denomination's next major flap coincided once again with external pressures from the wider world. For thousands of Christian Reformed GIs returning from the war, the world had become bigger, and their horizons were further expanded through the opportunity to attend college under the GI Bill. By the 1950s the walls of the ecclesiastical fortress built by the CRC appeared to be cracking, allowing new influences to seep in.

Once again, Calvin Seminary faculty found themselves the focus of significant quarreling as the denomination grappled with the "communist menace" in the East. By this time the neo-orthodoxy of Karl Barth had become a major player in theology and was being promoted in many seminaries and universities worldwide. Perhaps it was this influence that led some Calvin faculty members to suggest the formation of a Ph.D. program at Calvin as a way to keep future seminary professors safe through an in-house education from start to finish. Others on the faculty disagreed fiercely, deeming this a very un-Reformed approach to the world. In any case, the faculty was so completely at odds with itself that Synod 1952 made the extraordinary move of sacking nearly the entire teaching staff at Calvin Seminary.

Although this severe move brought more peace to the seminary community, disagreements continued elsewhere. *The Reformed Journal,* founded in 1951, gave voice to the more progressive, optimistic, Kuyperian wing of the CRC; *Torch and Trumpet,* founded one month later, was the forum for expressing a more reflexive case for the tradition. As the 1950s progressed, the *Reformed Journal* repeatedly pleaded for theological creativity and the freedom for theologians to explore new angles on old truths; *Torch and Trumpet* criticized such a stand, seeing it as a threat to orthodoxy and the purity of doctrine, to which the church had to adhere with all its strength.

By the time the CRC celebrated its centennial in 1957, it was able to look back at a varied history full of triumphs and steady growth that bore loving witness to the grace of God. But it could not avoid noting moments that were sobering and sad too. The church that had been formed out of multiple secessions had suffered a split of its own. The Christian Reformed community was perceived by some as being combative and occasionally mean-spirited, sacrificing love for the sake of fierce adherence to the tradition. Perhaps that explains in part the theme of the centennial celebration: "God's Favor Is Our Challenge." Many contended that by the grace of God, the CRC had been given a very refined doctrine. So in his lead article in the April 3, 1957, centennial celebration issue of *The Banner,* Marvin J. Vanderwerp laid out the very first prerequisite of meeting the challenge of God's favor: "a sincere concern for the truth." Vanderwerp went on to claim, rightly, that the very existence of the CRC as a denomination "is fundamentally a matter of doctrine." Looking toward the future, Vanderwerp contended that the CRC would not survive unless there was a revival of teaching doctrine to the youth and making their parents as enthusiastic about such matters as earlier generations had been. On that same page, Henry Schultze similarly claimed that Christian education is what enabled the CRC to survive as long as it had: "Throughout the years we as a church have been able, under God, to remain true to our basic confessions chiefly through the sustained teachings of our Christian schools. Our distinctiveness has been preserved for us largely by the work done in our school rooms."

Centennial edition of *The Banner,* 1957

One hundred years after the CRC had been founded as a move away from those perceived to be watering down the Reformed tradition, the writers celebrating the 1957 anniversary demonstrated by their words how deeply ingrained the desire for doctrinal purity remained. The intellectual rigor required to do that in an ever-changing world has always been and still remains one of the CRC's greatest strengths.

The apostle Paul said that those who are strong must lovingly bear with those who are weak. If the CRC's first hundred years proved anything, it was precisely how difficult that is to do, especially when each side of any given dispute is certain that it is the strong one! But if in 1957 the members of the CRC thought they had persevered through a century of tremendous change, they were right. What they could not have imagined was that the changes of the first hundred years were just a foretaste of the incredible changes the next fifty years would bring. To that more recent part of the story we now turn.

# THE CRC IN CANADA

I n the spring of 2005, I was on my way to Ottawa to give some lectures as part of a clergy conference. That trip seemed like the perfect time to read Tymen Hofman's fine book *The Canadian Story of the CRC: Its First Century.* Coming of age as I did in the 1970s and 80s, it was natural to assume that the Christian Reformed Church in North America had been a vigorous binational denomination for a very long time. As Hofman's history demonstrates, however, the full budding and flowering of the CRCNA in Canada is very much a story of the last half-century.

Much of the development of the CRC in Canada was a product of the events that followed World War II. Indeed, as I read Hofman's book while sitting in airports in Grand Rapids and then Chicago, I learned more about the key role played by Canadian troops in the liberation of the Netherlands from the Nazis. Not long after arriving in Ottawa, my Canadian host took me on a tour of the capital city. As it happened, the annual Tulip Festival was taking place throughout Ottawa—the streets and sidewalks teemed with tourists from all over Canada who had come to see the colorful flower beds that blanket the city each May. My host told me, "As you may know, Canada had a lot to do with freeing Holland from Hitler's grasp. So ever since, out of gratitude, the Dutch government has donated 1 million tulip bulbs a year to our city."

Beyond flowers, however, the result of Canada's role in liberating the Dutch from those dark years of Nazi occupation came principally in the form of a tidal wave of Dutch immigration to Canada in the years after the war. When those immigrants arrived on Canada's shores, many of them walked into the welcoming embrace of Christian Reformed pastors and congregations who were eager to enfold these newcomers into their church communities.

## The Beginning

The larger story, however, goes back to the very beginning of the twentieth century. As noted earlier in this book, the CRC came into existence in 1857 but remained a rather shaky, none-too-robust enterprise for the next few decades. For a while it seemed as though the fledgling denomination had all it could do to stay intact. Not surprisingly, therefore, the focus tended to remain inward for a time. But by the late 1800s, the denomination had stabilized sufficiently that many began to look outward to areas of mission and evangelism. Even as the theological school (and later also the college) was being organized in Grand Rapids, the CRC began its first formal mission effort in 1896 by establishing a ministry to the Navajo and Zuni Indians living in New Mexico. By 1903 the work in the American Southwest had progressed sufficiently that the CRC was able to establish Rehoboth, its first-ever mission school near Gallup, New Mexico.

At almost this same time, in 1904, the Christian Reformed congregation in Manhattan, Montana, received some correspondence from a group of Christians living in the territory of Alberta, Canada. As there were no established churches anywhere near the settlements in Alberta, the settlers there asked the Manhattan congregation if they could "borrow" its pastor to come and perform some infant baptisms. The Manhattan congregation readily agreed and dispatched their pastor, James Holwerda, to minister to this emerging gathering of fellow believers. The trip must surely have been a rugged and tiring one as Holwerda traveled some 400 miles by rail to

Lethbridge and from there traversed another twenty miles by wagon before arriving at the Nijverdal settlement in early May 1905. For the next two weeks, Holwerda preached the Word to upwards of sixty people and performed at least two baptisms. On the return home to Montana, Holwerda carried with him a petition from the settlement to have a home missionary assigned to them.

By November of that same year, the CRC had responded to this request by sending Rev. Meindert Botbijl and Rev. Holwerda to the settlement under the auspices of Classis Orange City. On November 16, 1905, these two pastors formalized the establishment of Nijverdal Christian Reformed Church. Within six years, the congregation had grown sufficiently to warrant the building of two separate churches, one on the east side of the area and the other on the west side. The Nijverdal group became the Monarch and Granum congregations, which remain the oldest Canadian congregations in the CRCNA.

During the next thirty years leading up to World War II, Christian Reformed congregations continued to be established across Canada. Significant work began in Ontario, which saw the establishment of churches

The liberation of Eindhoven

First CRC, Hamilton, Ontario; organized 1929

in Sarnia, Chatham, and Hamilton. By 1926 a group was formalized in the far West of Canada in Vancouver; work had also begun to establish churches in Edmonton. All in all, by 1940 there were fourteen Canadian CRC congregations served by eight pastors. The Canadian flock included 455 families and some 2,275 members. As Hofman notes, however, prior to World War II, none of these fourteen congregations was particularly vibrant or large. By way of comparison, Hofman notes that at the time of the war, Classis Grandville in Michigan had almost as many families and members in just that single classis as in the whole of Canada. Congregations were principally supported financially by sponsoring congregations in the United States that were eager to see churches flourish in America's nearest neighbor to the north. Clearly, therefore, the story of the growth of the CRC in Canada takes place in large part during that remarkable period after the war ended in 1945.

As indicated earlier, Canada endeared itself to the Dutch people by playing a prominent role in Holland's liberation from the scourge of Nazi fascism in 1945. In the years that followed the war, many Europeans sought to start over in a new land, leaving behind the terrible memories and physical devastation wrought by the recent war. To many such Dutch immigrants, Canada promised the fresh start they longed for. The influx of immigrants was nearly staggering at times. For instance, in 1954 alone, a scant nine years after the war's conclusion, Canada welcomed no fewer than 20,000 Dutch immigrants.

In 1946-47, seeing an opportunity to expand the CRC in Canada, church leaders established the "Immigration Committee for Canada"—a body that would continue to exist until 1966. Serving under the auspices of the CRC's Committee for Home Missions, the ICC received formal synodical authorization in 1947 and was granted regular funding through offerings taken in CRC congregations. Under the able leadership of Rev. Peter J. Hoekstra, the

ICC became a ministry of both word and deed. Immigrants were welcomed to Canada by members of the committee and by the many "field men" dispatched as home missionaries throughout Canada. Under the supervision of missionary-at-large John M. Vande Kieft, these field men assisted new immigrants in eminently practical ways, finding adequate housing and giving advice about finding meaningful employment. But the practical was always yoked to the spiritual; even as the ICC workers eased the immigrants' transition to a new nation, they also were in a position to ease them into new church homes. In cooperation with the Canadian government, Vande Kieft and others were eventually able to be part of the formal Canadian welcoming troupe, receiving passenger lists from the authorities and then actually meeting ships at harbors in Quebec and Halifax. Although these men worked with many people who never became part of the CRC in Canada, they clearly were key influences in steering a vast number of immigrants into established congregations.

"Field men" employed by the Immigration Committee for Canada

By 1954 the number of such people being ushered into the CRC had grown so much that it was no longer feasible simply to assimilate them into the congregations already in existence. Clearly the denomination needed many more new church plants to accommodate the burgeoning population of Dutch immigrants. In 1954, no fewer than twenty-three new congregations were established, making that year the zenith of church-planting in Canada. Such work continued unabated for a remarkable twenty years. As a result, the CRC in Canada grew from just fourteen established congregations in 1946 to 170 congregations by 1966, with a membership growth so large that by the mid-1960s, Canada comprised 27 percent of the CRCNA.

Although this meteoric growth in the Canadian CRC was clearly the result of an unprecedented wave of Dutch immigration, it is just as clear that there was nothing inevitable or automatic about it. That explosion in membership was the blessed result of much prayer and a lot of good old-fashioned hard work on the part of the ICC, the many field men, and the loving financial and prayer support provided by established congregations in both Canada and the United States.

## Tensions and New Growth

Mention the phrase "growing pains," and most people know instinctively what those words mean. With the lovely prospect of new growth comes the inevitable painful adjustments and realignments. So it was in Canada at mid-century: along with the joy of creating all those new congregations came the reality of finding sufficient numbers of pastors to lead them. Not surprisingly, the denomination was by no means able to keep pace by providing new pastors trained at Calvin Theological Seminary. Hence, from 1952 to 1961 Canadian congregations began bringing in pastors from other denominations, often directly from the Netherlands.

In Christian Reformed polity (or Church Order), the way for someone already ordained in another denomination to gain ordained status in the CRC is by sustaining a kind of "exam" called *colloquium doctum,* which is really more of a theological conversation in which the candidate displays his familiarity with the CRC as well as his assent to CRC doctrines, teachings, and practices. The first Dutch pastor who entered the CRC in Canada via this route was Rev. Gerard Bouma. Originally ordained as pastor of a Dutch congregation in Capelle a/d IJssel, Bouma sustained his *colloquium doctum* in Classis Chatham in 1952, after the CRC congregation in Essex, Ontario, had called him to become their new pastor. Forty-two other pastors would follow Bouma in entering the CRC by this route over the next nine years.

Gerard Bouma

This eased the shortage of pastors in Canada during that critical period of rapid growth. However, some CRC folk voiced concern over the language barrier, as worship in English was becoming the norm throughout the CRC at that time. Although some of the older Dutch pastors who came to Canada struggled with this new setting and tongue, most were able to adjust successfully. These transplanted Dutch pastors gave Canadian congregations a fresh infusion of the culture of the CRC's mother country. Thus, while many Christian Reformed congregations in the United States were becoming further removed from the old country, their Canadian counterparts maintained vibrant ties to the Netherlands.

These closer, more recent ties to Europe and to the Netherlands specifically, would become an identifying characteristic of Canadian members of the CRCNA. They may also have contributed to some of the differences in outlook between American congregations and their Canadian counterparts. As Tymen Hofman notes, Canadian delegates to the denomination's annual synod were often identified by "their distinct Canadian accents and Dutch brogues" [that] made them stand out as a growing element in the denomination" (Hofman, p. 113). But beyond such characteristic intonations, however, the Canadian wing of the CRCNA began to contribute valuable perspectives and ministry initiatives that have added to the denomination's diversity of ministries.

## Ministry and Education Initiatives

Because of the rapid growth of the Canadian churches, the CRCNA became a truly binational denomination by the end of the twentieth century. But despite the overall unity of the denomination and the similarity in doctrine, worship styles, and history on both sides of the border, the CRC in Canada developed its own unique character and made, therefore, its own unique contributions to the wider body. Some of this can be traced to the different form of government that exists in Canada and hence the different relationship that churches have to the authorities vis-à-vis churches in the United States. Other Canadian contributions to the broader CRCNA tie in with initiatives in education—both elementary and high schools as well as institutes of higher learning.

Members of the CRC in Canada have long been active in organizing movements in education, labor, and agriculture. One of the more significant developments in higher education over the last forty years began in the

1950s when a coalition of interested parties formed the Association for Reformed Scientific Scholarship, later called Association for the Advancement of Christian Scholarship. This group had the ambitious goal of establishing a Christian university in Canada; they moved closer to this dream in 1965 when Dr. Paul Schrotenboer was hired as director of AACS and charged with the mandate of opening a school as soon as was feasible.

Just two years later the Institute for Christian Studies was formally established in Toronto with Dr. Hendrik Hart as its first professor of philosophy. Although a very small operation initially (and without the ability to grant degrees), ICS grew rapidly. By 1972 the school had moved to a new location and was able to provide masters degree programs of study in philosophy. Subsequent collaborations with the Free University in Amsterdam allowed students to work toward Ph.D. degrees (granted by the Free University but worked on largely at ICS) even as additional masters programs were added to the ICS curriculum.

Institute for Christian Studies, Toronto

As an overtly Christian and Reformed school, ICS has continued to shape a Christian worldview through an interdisciplinary approach to learning. In wider, specifically Christian Reformed circles, however, ICS became known for its attachment to the teachings of the Dutch scholar Herman Dooyeweerd, whose philosophical stances and approaches to culture and the world were not universally hailed as representing the essence of a Reformed approach. According to Hofman, there were periods of some tension between ICS and Calvin College, particularly between the philosophy departments of the two schools.

Not everyone in either Canada or the U.S. was enthusiastic about the ICS approach to faith and learning. But despite these differences, the institution itself has continued to move forward in significant ways. In 2005 ICS President Harry Fernhout, who had served since 1990, left to become president of The King's University College and was succeeded in 2006 by John Suk. At about this same time, ICS received permission to begin granting its own Ph.D. degrees in philosophy, making ICS one of the first-ever privately funded Christian colleges in Canada with this ability.

But ICS is not alone in representing excellence in Christian higher education in Canada. In 1979 seventy-six students enrolled at the newly opened King's University College in Edmonton, Alberta. Within fifteen years King's had become a firmly established institution with a student body of almost 600 students and, as of 1993, King's occupied a spacious new campus on which to carry out its educational work. Over the years, King's has benefited from a good relationship with the University of Alberta, whose resources have been opened to King's students even as the larger university accepted the transfer of educational credits from King's for any students who continued their studies there.

One year after the inauguration of King's, the establishing of Redeemer University College was approved. Redeemer formally opened its doors on the other side of Canada in September 1982 with an initial student body of some ninety full-time and sixty-three part-time students. After meeting for quite a few years in temporary facilities in Hamilton, Ontario, the school eventually moved to a spacious and beautiful new campus built on seventy-eight acres of land in nearby Ancaster. Under the guidance of President Henry DeBolster and more recently Justin Cooper, Redeemer's student population has climbed steadily and is now home to nearly 800 students.

Beyond education, the Christian Reformed presence in Canada has been manifested in other ways as well. Although not formally affiliated with nor sponsored by the CRC, Canadian church leaders became active in promoting the Christian Labour Association in Canada, Citizens for Public Justice, and the Christian Farmers Federation of Ontario. These and other similar organizations were good examples of a Reformed approach to culture and society, expressing tangibly a larger sense of vocation, of carrying out God's designs for life in all areas of society and at all levels. Although such organizations were not run by the church, they embodied Calvinist ideals and principles readily apparent in the abiding concern participants displayed for justice and for proper sustainability for those engaged in agriculture.

As longtime Canadian Ministries Director William Veenstra wrote to me, the Canadian members of the CRCNA have a rich history of seeking to have a "transformational influence" on Canadian culture. In addition to the agencies just mentioned and to the formation of schools at every level of education, Canadian Christian Reformed churches have also engaged in ecumenical endeavors sponsored by the Canadian Council of Churches and the Evangelical Fellowship of Canada. Through such involvements, Canadian churches have launched outreach ministries to a wide variety of people in a wide variety of circumstances including campus ministries at many of

Christian Labour Association of Canada

Canada's major universities, seafarers ministries at the ports of Vancouver and Montreal, and ministries to First Nations people in places such as Winnipeg, Regina, and Edmonton.

In all of these ways, the Canadian wing of the CRC has left its own distinctive and indelible mark on the denomination and on the Canadian culture. Being a binational denomination certainly presents its own set of challenges in terms of structure

and governance (see below). But these pale in significance compared to the great riches of ministry blessings that accumulate when people of both nations together share a common desire to bring all things under the lordship of Jesus Christ. To paraphrase Abraham Kuyper's most famous phrase, there is not one square inch in all creation of which Christ Jesus cannot say, "That is mine!" Thanks to its binational character, the CRC has been able to apply that inspiring message to the whole of North America, from Smithers to Miami, from Halifax to San Diego, and every square inch in between!

## Living as One

As even this brief summary makes clear, the remarkable story of the CRC in Canada has added much to the overall character and richness of the CRCNA. However, the binational character of the denomination has not been without its difficulties. Structurally there has always been the need for a sense of true parity and equality between the two nations that the CRCNA calls home. Canadian congregations have properly wanted to have their own voice in major decisions, particularly ones that directly affected the

GAYLA POSTMA

Bikers touch their wheels in the Atlantic at Halifax

Canadian wing of the denomination. But because traditionally much of the church's bureaucracy has been located in Grand Rapids, Michigan, there was always the lingering fear that even the Canadian part of the CRCNA was being run from afar (and by American leaders at that).

Over the years various scenarios and structural concepts have been suggested and implemented to ease such tensions and to help the denomination preserve its unity while at the same time recognizing its binationality. Around the time of the denomination's centennial celebration in 1957, serious consideration was given to the idea of Canadian "regional synods," which perhaps could give a fuller expression of the Canadian viewpoint and identity in denominational decision-making. This idea was never formally approved or adopted. However, because efforts in this direction persisted into the mid-1960s, synod did eventually approve the formation of the Council of Christian Reformed Churches in Canada (CCRCC), which came into existence in 1968. Each Canadian classis delegated representatives to an annual meeting at which Canada-specific issues were dealt with in ways more expedient than could have been accomplished at the wider synod.

By 2000, however, the entire CRCNA was reassessing its structure, and when a new denominational plan was adopted by the synod, the need for the CCRCC was eliminated in favor of a larger Board of Trustees for the denomination to be comprised of one-half Canadian trustees and one-half American. A similar parity was to exist on other major denominational boards and committees so as to promote, as much as possible, unity amidst the diversity inherent in a binational church.

Even as the CRCNA prepared to celebrate its sesquicentennial in 2007, the Canadian branch of the denomination marked its centennial in 2005. Among the festivities that celebrated God's faithfulness in the Canadian CRC was the "Sea to Sea" bike tour in the summer of 2005. Traveling for over two months from Vancouver, British Columbia, all the way to Halifax, Nova Scotia, cyclists covered just over 7,000 kilometers (4,200 miles) on what was hailed as the longest bike trip ever across the Canadian nation. Organizers, led by the man who first dreamed of such a trip, Al Karsten, believed the celebratory tour would be a wonderful way to remind Canadians of God's faithfulness across a century and to encourage everyone to give God the glory for all God had done and made possible. At the tour's conclusion, the cyclists who had first dipped their back tires into the waters of the Pacific Ocean off British Columbia dipped their front tires into the Atlantic off the coast of Nova Scotia. (One cyclist is reported to have thrown his entire bike into the Atlantic!) What followed was a grand worship celebration of praise for God's faithfulness to the CRC in Canada—a faithfulness that extends not just from "sea to sea" but from generation to generation. And that is a chorus of praise all Christian Reformed members, Canadian and American alike, may joyfully join!

# AND WITH ALL YOUR MIND:
# THE WORK OF SYNOD

I n one of Flannery O'Connor's vivid, even startling stories, a devout older woman is desperately trying to reach out to a cynical, bitter teenager. At one point the woman plaintively informs the young man, "Jesus died for your sins!"

"I never ast him," the boy snaps back.

In a way, this old woman's evangelistic appeal and the boy's sneering reply of disbelief summarize an issue that consumed the Christian Reformed Church for nearly half of the 1960s. By the early 1960s, the monthly *Reformed Journal* had become a respected voice for the more progressive strain of Reformed thought in North America. Founded in 1951 by James Daane, Harry Boer, and Henry Stob, the *Journal* forthrightly tried to enliven and enlarge the Reformed voice in reaction to what the editors believed had been a long period of insularity and defensiveness within Reformed circles.

Labeling the theology of the recent past as sterile, commonplace, and repetitious, Daane asserted that *The Reformed Journal* would become a showplace for "a Reformed theology bristling with vitality and restless with creative power" (RJ 1, Sept. 1951, quoted in Bratt, p. 193). The magazine that Daane and others formed lived up to this reputation in articles that regularly sparred with the more conservative voices of *Torch and Trumpet,* as well as the CRC's official publication *The Banner.*

James Daane, one of the founders of *Reformed Journal*

Daane wanted a theology "bristling with vitality"—but from time to time articles in the *Journal* caused some in the denomination to bristle in an altogether different way. In December 1962, Calvin Theological Seminary professor of missions Harold Dekker published "God So Loves . . . All Men," an article that called for a reassessment of "limited atonement," a key theological tenet of the Reformed tradition. As spelled out most extensively in the CRC's confessional statement "The Canons of Dort," the atonement worked by Jesus on the cross was "limited" in the sense that it was intended only for those who had already been elected by God to be saved. Although claiming that the value of Christ's sacrifice "is of infinite worth, more than sufficient to atone for the sins of the whole world" (Art. 3), the CRC had long confessed that the only people who would ever benefit from this saving death (and the only ones ever even intended by God to so benefit) were those whom God had elected in the secret counsels of his divine providence. The Canons of Dort explicitly rejected the idea that Jesus' death made available a salvation that anyone could tap into if they chose to believe in Jesus. Salvation was not available for just anybody and had nothing to do with human choice. Salvation came as a result of *God's* choice in electing who would be saved through the death of God's Son.

In his 1962 article, followed up by several others in succeeding months, Professor Dekker wondered why the CRC had not been more successful on the mission field over the years. Many people had long lamented the CRC's slow growth on both the domestic mission front as well as overseas. Dekker believed he had perhaps hit on a partial answer: perhaps the reason the CRC did not gain more converts was because it was not trying hard enough, and perhaps the reason it was not trying harder was because the CRC had such a shrunken, restricted view of God's love that Christian Reformed missionaries were not always sure what they could offer the average non-Christian in the first place. Dekker noted that mission workers from other denominations were able to come up to even a total stranger and say, "Christ died for you," thereby extending a genuine invitation for this person to believe in the Jesus who had sacrificed himself for this person. Dekker argued that the CRC's limited view of God's love (restricted to those already elected to be saved) meant that Reformed folks could not really say "Christ

Harold Dekker

died for you" because they could never be sure this was true. If a given individual turned out not to be among the elect, then it would be false to claim "Christ died for you."

Hence, since one could never be sure precisely where the love of God applied and where it did not, the CRC's mission and witness efforts had become altogether too hesitant. In presenting this, Dekker strenuously avoided the free-will approach of the so-called "Arminians" who claimed that the salvation of a person's soul begins the moment that person, on his or her own, decides to follow Jesus. Dekker was careful to maintain the doctrine of salvation by grace alone by consistently saying it was always the hidden, prior working of God's Holy Spirit that moved people to receive the faith by which conversion took place. In this way, salvation remained completely God's doing and was not dependent on any human act or choice.

Still, as a professor dedicated to the mission zeal of the CRC, Dekker wanted to find a way to expand the denomination's view of God's love such that one could believe God really does love all people. Dekker wanted to find a way to be able to approach any and all with genuine fervor, to be able to say "Christ died for you" without having to hedge that promise by off-putting and unwieldy theological provisos and caveats.

But a great many people in the denomination did not love Dekker's version of God's love. His articles elicited a firestorm of protest from those who sincerely believed that a major piece of Reformed theology was in danger of being destroyed (by a professor at the denomination's official seminary, at that). After nearly eighteen months, during which a flurry of articles and counter-articles appeared in all of the magazines associated with the CRC, Synod 1964 appointed a study committee with a daunting mandate: by Synod 1966 the committee was to bring forward a biblical and confessional study that would relate the notion of "limited atonement" to the teachings currently being promulgated by Professor Dekker.

Two years later the committee, led by Dr. John H. Bratt, presented a seventy-page report that, if nothing else, bore witness to the historical fact that many of the Reformed tradition's central teachings traffic deep in the mysteries of God's providence and decrees. Caught up in the current questions of God's love and the extent of that love toward a fallen creation were far more dicey and tangled questions about God's election, as well as what even the study committee labeled as the "ghosts" of 1924 when the CRC dealt with the "common grace" of God. That earlier controversy had led to a schismatic split when those who disagreed with the idea that some form of God's grace comes to all people left the CRC to form the Protestant Reformed denomination. Ever since, applying God's grace (or in this case God's love) more broadly than to Christians alone had remained a sensitive topic within the CRC.

In the end the study committee emphasized the mysteries of God's will in their report to Synod 1966. They affirmed the traditional teaching of limited atonement while at the same time recognizing that our finite minds may simply be unable to understand the apparent paradoxes involved in saying that Christ's sacrifice is sufficient for all, even though, in the end, it is not effective for all people. Furthermore, to avoid the potential theological mayhem that could be implied by the missionary invitation "Christ died for you," the committee opted for the broader, but theologically more nuanced, proclamation "Christ died for sinners." That phrasing was not only theologically uncontroversial, it gave the missionary the chance to do an internal

shrug of the shoulders regarding the question of whether or not this particular sinner was among the elect and would thus gain salvation through from
Christ's saving death.

Obviously the committee also needed to deal with the status of Professor
Dekker (with whom they had had contact and correspondence). The study
report itself did not make any overt admonishments to Professor Dekker
directly. But it did assert that the language of "Christ died for you" was inap-
propriate for a Reformed missionary to use, and that, furthermore, the
Reformed notion of a limited atonement is actually an incentive for, not a
hindrance to, mission work. By implication, then, the committee called upon
the professor to reassess and the restate his prior claims.

The committee's rigorous work was, in the end, a kind of "both/and"
approach that tried to affirm traditional teachings while at the same time recognizing that we may never understand some of the mysteries of God's
work.

Unhappily for the committee, however, their work proved unacceptable
to Synod 1966. After extensive debate, the entire matter was sent back to the
committee with an updated mandate to bring back an expanded and restat-
ed report to synod the following year. Synodical delegates believed that the
"confusing state of contemporary theology" (*Acts* 1966, p. 69) meant that this
matter needed far more biblical and confessional support than either the
study committee or synod's own advisory committee were able to provide.

By the time Synod 1967 convened, matters had grown even more tense.
Over two dozen overtures were submitted by various classes and congregations, many calling for a postponement of any action in favor of further
study, some demanding that a definitive stance be taken regarding the status of Professor Dekker, and a couple calling for Dekker's suspension from
his duties at Calvin Seminary. Meanwhile, Dekker himself submitted a
lengthy reply to the 1966 study committee report. For its part, in 1967 the
study committee turned in a revised report that now had been expanded to
ninety-four pages. Although the substance of the report remained the same,
the committee added (as had been requested the previous year) numerous
biblical references, more extensive conversation with theologians and the
church's confessions, and an Appendix dealing with some related issues.

But once again synod found itself essentially at an impasse on this issue.
On Friday, June 23, the ninth day of Synod 1967, the advisory committee was
finally ready to make its recommendations. Their report was received and

commended to the churches as a valuable resource for study on questions relating to the scope of God's love and of Christ's atoning work. But when it came to making declarations about the controversy itself, the advisory committee could not agree, and so presented two sets of recommendations to the delegates, reflecting the seven to six split among the advisory committee's thirteen members. The first recommendation put before synod on that Friday proved to be the only one that would be considered that week. Backed by extensive biblical and confessional support, the committee asked synod to declare that "it is unwarranted to say 'That God loves all men with a redemptive love'" (*Acts* 1967, p. 100).

The debate that followed made it clear that this matter was far from being settled. In an extraordinary move, on Saturday morning when the delegates reconvened, they were informed that Synod 1967 would recess for two months, reconvening in Grand Rapids on August 29. Yet another committee was appointed to try to bring together all the parties and all the disparate recommendations in the hopes that when synod reconstituted itself in August, this snarled matter could be brought to a reasonable conclusion.

On Tuesday morning, August 29, President William Haverkamp (who would note the dubious distinction of having been the active president of synod longer than anyone else in history) welcomed the delegates back and urged them to carry out their "responsible task" in dependence on the Holy Spirit and in the same "brotherly spirit which marked our earlier sessions" (*Acts* 1967, p. 728). The debate would continue throughout that day and for the entire day on Wednesday, August 30, as well.

Strikingly, as James Bratt notes, in the end this mountain of synodical labor produced only a molehill of a decision (Bratt, p. 207). After bringing forward, but then tabling and re-tabling one set of recommendations after another, the officers of synod forced the study committee and the advisory committee to come to one last unified recommendation, which was at long last adopted: "That Synod admonish Professor Dekker for the ambiguous and abstract way in which he has expressed himself in his writing on the love of God and the atonement" (*Acts* 1967, p. 736).

After three years of extensive synodical work, in the end the church's official teachings remained unchanged. And the man in the center of this doctrinal hurricane was admonished for not writing out his thoughts more clearly, which seemed to be an implicit way of saying that there was room within the denomination for Professor Dekker's viewpoints, provided they were not presented too abstractly or confusingly.

Although perhaps a less-than-elegant or satisfactory conclusion, this first major synodical and denominational controversy of the last half century demonstrates something of the CRC's historic strengths. The rigorous scholarship that went into studying "the love of God," as well as the thoughtful combination of pastoral concern and theological scholarship that was behind Harold Dekker's initial article to begin with, reveal much about the Christian Reformed mind. At their best, synodical study committees exhibit both an uncompromising intellectual rigor rooted in biblical studies and a humble willingness to accept the limits of our knowledge when faced with the mysteries of an infinite God.

There is even strength in the willingness to embrace the tensions in apparent paradoxes instead of forever seeking to relax every tension in the vain belief that we already know all there is to know. This openness to mystery and the willingness to admit that we will never be finished returning to God's Word to see what we have missed (or even misunderstood) is always in competition with the desire to settle everything quickly and in tidy black-and-white formulations. Also, as is evident in this protracted synodical debate, the laudable desire to be intellectually rigorous can become a liability when rigor eclipses humility, that is, remaining lovingly open toward those whose positions may vary (however slightly) from our own. But when openness, humility, intellectual rigor, and a love of study are all held together in creative tension, the CRC has found it possible to produce a highly respected level of biblical and theological scholarship. In this particular case perhaps no one was satisfied in the end. But that too happens sometimes when the height, breadth, and depth of difficult matters are explored honestly and thoroughly.

Meanwhile, as controversy raged within the CRC, the outside world was careening through the tumultuous sixties. Ironically, on June 23, 1967—the very day synod took up the love of God debate once again—the Beatles released a new song. And by the end of August, when Synod 1967 reconvened, "All You Need Is Love" had soared to become a number one hit worldwide. It was a message people needed and wanted in the midst of that war-torn, racially charged, and violent decade. Even as the delegates in Calvin College's brand new Fine Arts Center scrutinized the extent of God's love, millions of people around the world were listening to John Lennon sing,

"There's nothing you can make that can't be made, no one you can save that can't be saved. It's easy. All you need is love." In an odd way, perhaps that was what Harold Dekker had been suggesting all along, too.

## A Lamp unto Our Feet: Scripture's Authority

People tend to mark off historical epochs in convenient blocks of time like centuries and decades. The 1960s is generally remembered as a decade of turmoil and unrest. Thus Vietnam, the hippie culture, the assassinations of key leaders like the Kennedys, Malcolm X, and Martin Luther King, Jr., are all restricted in our collective consciousness to the sixties. We forget that those events had significant carryover into those early years of the 1970s. The war in Vietnam did not end until 1975 (and then ignominiously). Meanwhile, the Nixon White House slowly rattled apart through the Watergate scandals that began in 1972 and were finally resolved in 1974 (again, ignominiously) when Richard Nixon became the first president ever to resign from office.

At the same time during the early 1970s, however, synod was engaged in significant study that produced a remarkable set of documents. In 1971 and 1972 synod considered a report on "The Nature and Extent of Biblical Authority." By 1973 synod had received not less than three substantial reports dealing with homosexuality, with the neo-Pentecostal phenomenon, and with the nature of ordained office in the church (the latter report would ultimately play a role in what may be the most significant synodical story of the last thirty years: the ordination of women to the offices of the church). That such a prodigious volume of scholarship could have been generated within the span of only a few years is a testament to the CRC's commitment to ongoing study of God's Word. At the very least, each of the reports just mentioned warrants a summary of its findings, conclusions, and recommendations.

"The Nature and Extent of Biblical Authority" touches the heart of the Reformed tradition and its core commitment to the integrity of God's Word and to the utter necessity for God to reveal himself to us through that Word. In what ultimately became known as "Report 44," a synodical study committee addressed, in a pastoral yet intellectually rigorous way, a number of questions that had arisen on the authority of Scripture. Since a good deal of the more liberal scholarship on such questions originated in Europe, it is perhaps not surprising that at least some of the concerns on biblical matters filtered into the CRC via its connections to the mother church in the Netherlands as well as through organizations like the Reformed Ecumenical Synod (later called Reformed Ecumenical Council), which was comprised of many members with strong ties to Europe.

Theological issues in this area can get very complex very quickly, such that even attempting a brief summary is difficult. Because the study committee, led by Calvin Seminary professor Andrew Bandstra, saw itself as a servant of the church, committee members struggled to engage the relevant questions in a thorough way yet without becoming so technical as to render their report unintelligible to rank and file members of the denomination. In general, it can be said that, starting in the nineteenth century, some theologians had begun to question what may be the very foundation of the Christian faith; namely, God's revelation to humanity in the Bible.

Andrew Bandstra

Traditionally the first systematic theology course most seminary students take is called "Prolegomena," which teaches the doctrine of revelation and thus studies how Scripture is the revealed Word of God. Students must start here because if there is no reliable way to know the truths of God and of God's Word in the first place, then the rest of theology totters. Take away God's Word, and the rest of theology has nothing on which to build and so nowhere to go. Prolegomena lays the foundation for all that follows.

It was precisely this foundation that many scholars, especially in Europe and specifically in Germany, began to question. Some wondered what it means to say that the Bible is God's Word. How can we know it is divinely inspired, and what would such inspiration entail? Still others said that even to the extent that Scripture can be said to have a divine origin, how does that belief control the church's interpretation of any given text? Is there a so-called "canon within the canon"? That is, are some parts of the Bible more

Synod 1969 launched a new study committee to address core issues related to
the Bible

inspired—or at least more relevant for salvation through Christ—than others? Do some parts of the Bible seem less divine than others? Can we adhere to Scripture as God's Word even if we say that some parts of the Bible can be interpreted figuratively whereas other portions must be taken literally? Or must one interpret every passage the same way, taking each as literal truth without distinction?

Given the advances in science that had taken place starting in the days of John Calvin and Martin Luther, perceptions of the nature of the universe and its origins began to change, casting into doubt for many the nature of the text in Genesis. How could Genesis be read and interpreted as God's Word if the long-held literalistic reading of it no longer accorded with scientific evidence? And if the nature of the text in Genesis changed from literal to something more symbolic or figurative, what was to prevent the same change in status for other parts of the Bible (even for passages as vital to the faith as the resurrection story in the four gospels)?

Questions such as these weighed heavily on the minds of scholars around the world. But because these issues touched on nothing less than the Bible—and the nature of well-known, much-loved Sunday school stories at that—this was one area of theological scholarship that engaged the minds and hearts of lay people as well. So Synod 1969 launched a new study committee to address these core issues related to the Word of God. As noted above, this committee was formed mainly in reaction to developments in the Netherlands and in the Reformed Ecumenical Synod, which had requested member denominations to provide guidance and study on this matter. But the CRC had in-house reasons for addressing this as well, including concerns that some had raised about the teaching of certain Calvin College professors, chiefly Dr. Willis DeBoer, whose ideas on the early chapters of Genesis had caused some consternation.

The study committee consisted of a number of eminent Christian Reformed scholars, some of whom were Calvin College professors and others who were (or would later become) professors at Calvin Theological Seminary: Andrew Bandstra (chair), John G. Groen, David Holwerda, Fred Klooster, Jack Vos (not a faculty member of either institution), Marten Woudstra, and reporter/author Gordon Spykman.

From the outset there had been an overriding concern not to treat Scripture in a "dualistic" way. The Bible was to be approached as a unified whole, and interpreted as such from start to finish. There was a strong desire to avoid the impression of claiming that some parts of the Bible are more important, more inspired, more divine, or more literal than other parts. As the committee stated early in its initial report, "Although obviously it is necessary to make some distinctions in interpreting concrete expressions of Scripture's authority . . . any attempt to separate in a dualistic fashion the content of Scripture from the form in which it comes to us runs counter to the genius of the Reformed tradition" (*Acts* 1971, p. 463).

The report went on to affirm that we may claim the Bible as God's authoritative Word because its origin lies solely with God through the Holy Spirit and because the whole of Scripture ultimately witnesses to and presents redemption through Christ Jesus the Lord. Whether narrating the history that led up to the advent of Jesus or detailing the events and meaning of Christ's sacrificial life, the whole of the Bible authoritatively tells us the truth about creation, fall, and redemption.

There was no doubt in the report that the Bible speaks authoritatively to the whole of human life in God's creation. What remained to be explored, therefore, was how a given passage or type of biblical literature accomplished this task. In good Reformed fashion, the committee highlighted what is sometimes called the "organic" nature of inspiration. The Bible as a whole did not drop into anyone's lap out of a clear blue sky, nor did any individual passage or book in the Bible. Instead, any given passage of the Bible was the work of a human author who lived in a concrete time and place and who wrote, under the direct inspiration of the Spirit, from that specific time and place through the use of the author's own style and skill.

This view of inspiration implies that certain historical and cultural ideas may be reflected in a biblical passage without being considered once-for-all views that all subsequent readers of the Bible must accept along with the Bible's larger redemptive message. For example, the report mentioned that for a long time people in the Western world have located the heart as the symbolic seat of human emotions, whereas most of the authors of the Bible, particularly in the Old Testament, believed that the bowels, the kidneys, or some other lower abdominal region was the "location" of human feelings. Despite the difference in views that may be reflected in a particular passage, we can still grant that passage an authoritative status as God's Word.

In general, the committee's report nicely displayed "the genius of the Reformed tradition" by repeatedly making a case for balance and nuance. The report nowhere compromised on Scripture as the inspired Word of God, but precisely because of that strong position it was able to build a thoughtful case for recognizing the ongoing validity of classic Reformed approaches to the Bible.

Biblical interpreters must always realize that any given text has both an original meaning for the time when the words were first written and an ongoing meaning with relevance that continues to us yet today. In terms of scientific discoveries that change our understanding of the creation, the committee adroitly noted that John Calvin himself was not unsettled by the Copernican discovery in his day that the earth revolved around the sun (and not the other way around). When some claimed that the Bible's apparent teaching that the sun went around the earth made it inaccurate, Calvin said that this was not a problem in that Moses (the traditional author of Genesis) was not doing astronomy when he composed the biblical text but was speaking to us in a theological way. Furthering our understanding of the universe through science, the committee said, is a proper exercise of the cultural mandate that God gave to Adam and Eve in the beginning.

God wants us to explore creation by using our minds. Subsequent discoveries may make us understand certain biblical passages somewhat differently than we once had, but what science can never do is dictate to any person of faith how the Bible must be interpreted. There is an important difference between having our larger understanding of the world expanded by science and having science call the shots in terms of what the Bible may or may not mean in terms of its redemptive message. Again, maintaining this fine balance is testament to the rigor and deep intelligence behind this landmark piece of work.

Two years after it began its work, the study committee submitted the fruit of its labor—Report 36—to Synod 1971. The final report represented a significant contribution to the church's larger understanding of the nature of biblical authority. Synod, however, decided to refer the report to the churches for study. Congregations and classes were encouraged to read the report and forward comments or suggestions for change to the committee. And read it they did! The original printing of just over 10,000 copies was exhausted in less than six months. By the time Synod 1972 met, the committee had received formal letters from ninety-seven consistories with an additional sixty-one letters from individual CRC members—more than sufficient input to warrant a significant re-working of the original draft.

In the end the report grew from thirty-six pages to fifty-three, and its five points of pastoral advice were expanded to seven. Portions of Report 36 that had caused confusion (particularly regarding the nature of Genesis 1-11) were removed or substantially reworked, even as some specific rejections of contrary or competing theories about Scripture were added for clarity. Concerns that the committee had, despite its disavowal of this very idea, presented a dualistic approach to the Bible were also directly addressed.

The resulting revised report came to Synod 1972 as Report 44. This report, and its seven points of pastoral advice, were adopted and commended to the congregations. The first of those seven points was intended to be as clear a statement as possible of where the CRC stood: "Synod calls the churches to a wholehearted recognition that Scripture addresses us with full divine authority as the saving revelation of God in Jesus Christ and that this authority applies to Scripture in its total extent and in all its parts" (*Acts* 1972, p. 545). This statement put a lot of daylight between the CRC and those who held out for "a canon within the canon" or any idea that only certain parts of the Bible needed to be seen as God's Word whereas others could be deemed non-essential or uninspired.

But it was perhaps the sixth point that would unwittingly set the stage for much of what was to come on the floor of synod for the balance of the twentieth century. Because the committee made clear that although it had established certain boundaries within which to carry out the task of biblical interpretation, even so a certain "freedom of biblical interpretation" needed to be honored and respected. This was the committee's way of noting that people of good faith can approach Scripture from the same starting point and with the same set of good interpretive tools but not necessarily arrive at the same interpretation. Respecting this point was deemed by the committee to be a "brotherly obligation" (*Acts* 1972, p. 546). Coming years, however, would put that fraternal spirit sorely to the test.

## Assessing Neo-Pentecostalism

As Synod 1972 concluded the CRC's significant look at the Bible's authority, three other study committees were finalizing their work. Since all three reports hit the floor of Synod 1973, the delegates that year faced a daunting challenge. In addition to the three major reports on Neo-Pentecostalism, homosexuality, and the nature of ordained office, Synod 1973 also received a report on the question of whether women could serve in the ordained offices of the church.

Those who were delegates at Synod 1973 will tell you that it was a landmark session. Whether or not the "Agenda for Synod" was the thickest such volume ever produced, it must have ranked near the top for sheer heft. For ten days, from June 12 to June 22, the delegates deliberated on a flurry of issues. Although this chapter can present only the merest summary of this work, it should be noted that much of Synod 1973's work has endured the test of time for the decades that have passed since.

No synodical report is ever perfect, nor are its recommendations ever perfectly carried out in the congregations. The issues dealt with in 1973 have been revisited (and, in the case of women in office, revised incessantly) but the bulk of that year's scholarship and pastoral advice has remained firmly in place.

A perennial criticism of the Reformed tradition—and of the CRC specifically—relates to a perceived lack of emphasis on the person and work of the Holy Spirit. Those who are minded to level this critique often point to the Heidelberg Catechism. Although this is undoubtedly the landmark summary of the Reformed tradition's teachings and beliefs, a surface reading of this confession reveals a dearth of words about the Spirit. Of course, as many have pointed out, a closer reading reveals the presence of the Holy Spirit pervasively throughout the Catechism, active in the providence of God, the sacraments of the church, the preaching of God's Word, the living out of the Christian faith, and in every prayer a Christian offers. Among the more well-known of John Calvin's doctrines is his teaching about "the inner testimony of the Holy Spirit" by which the truths of Scripture and the reality of God's presence are confirmed in the hearts of believers.

Even so, the Reformed tradition has never been described as charismatically over-enthusiastic or exuberant. Traditionally, worship in Reformed congregations has been more restrained—possessed of a deep and abiding joy to be sure, but this joy and the faith behind it were expressed in more intellectual and articulate ways: in the singing of psalms, in thoughtfully composed hymns, in heartfelt prayers, and above all in a rigorous form of doctrinal preaching rooted in well-exegeted biblical texts.

But while all that was characteristic of the Reformed tradition, a new wave of Pentecostalism was sweeping North America. Many trace the origins of so-called Neo-Pentecostalism to revivals held in the early twentieth century. Rooted in elements of the Holiness movements in the late nineteenth and early twentieth centuries, the modern explosion in Pentecostal churches came in the first years of the twentieth century when an emphasis on "baptism by the Holy Spirit" (proclaimed by holiness preachers like Charles Fox Parham and others) became yoked with the phenomenon of glossolalia, or speaking in tongues. Most historians trace one major stream of influence to a small church on Azusa Street in Los Angeles. Founded in an old stable in 1906 by a black preacher named William Joseph Seymour, the Azusa Street church became, in Martin E. Marty's characterization, "a second Jerusalem" with "Seymour [becoming] a new apostle" (Vol. 1, p. 244).

In coming years there would be an ever-increasing emphasis on the more spectacular (and, according to Neo-Pentecostals, also long-neglected) gifts of the Holy Spirit with tongues-speaking leading the way. By 1914 those promoting the baptism of the Holy Spirit and its attendant gifts began organizing. The Assemblies of God church traces its origins back to those years just prior to the outbreak of World War I. By the century's end, the Assemblies of God had exploded to nearly 12,000 congregations and over 2 million believers in the United States alone.

Neo-Pentecostalism's impact on the CRC was not immediate. By the 1960s and 70s, however, leaders in the CRCNA began to note that more and more Reformed people were finding elements of Neo-Pentecostalism highly attractive. The movement's emphasis on experience and on exuberant worship provided a striking alternative to the more staid practices of traditional Reformed worship. Many in the CRCNA found this merely baffling. The Neo-Pentecostal movement had long been criticized by Reformed leaders for what they saw as its lack of intellectual rigor and its simplistic approach to the Bible, and for some of the more bizarre practices to which at least fringe portions of the wider movement seemed perennially prone.

A portion of the 1973 study committee report on Neo-Pentecostalism was devoted to wondering why this particular movement seemed to be exercising a "widespread appeal to members of the Christian Reformed Church."

Azusa Street Mission, an influential center of
Neo-Pentecostalism

Among the committee's findings (based on interviews conducted with former CRC members who had joined the charismatic movement) was a stinging critique of the CRC's (perceived) lack of emphasis on spiritual power.
Some claimed that CRC members "gloried in our heritage, not in our Lord"
while others claimed they had found in Neo-Pentecostal worship services a
transforming power and joy that was all but wholly lacking in CRC services
that showed "a lack of originality . . . and vision" (*Agenda* 1973, pp. 407-07).

Inherent in many of those comments were sobering points of reflection
for those who remained in the CRC. Of course, as the committee's report
noted, people's hankering to belong to a denomination that was wildly different from the average CRC congregation was part and parcel of a wider
cultural move toward all that was novel. The CRC was not alone in witnessing an exodus of members leaving for the more dynamic congregations in the charismatic movement. Since the end of World War II, the
North American culture had undergone giant shifts and changes. A desire
to change also one's own spiritual experiences in the church was simply a
reflection of other tectonic shifts in people's sensibilities and expectations
in a society becoming more and more dominated by the entertainment
industry, and where individuals were increasingly driven to have fulfilling
personal experiences.

However, tracing the sociological and spiritual whys and wherefores of Neo-Pentecostalism's appeal was not the primary purpose of the 1973 report. The committee, chaired by Bassam Madany, included the report's author, John Stek, as well as other key denominational figures: Michael DeVries, Dirk Hart, David Holwerda, Leonard Sweetman, and Stuart Bergsma. In the end they submitted a report that ran to 101 pages, making it very nearly a book in its own right. In good Reformed fashion, a major section of the report was devoted to tracing out the person and work of the Holy Spirit as Scripture presented it and as the confessions of the Reformed tradition summarized that biblical witness. Naturally, the report lingered over specific questions as to the nature of the Spirit's gifts and particularly the nature of the more spectacular gifts that had not traditionally been exercised in Reformed congregation, but that had become the identifying hallmark of Neo-Pentecostal churches.

Among the questions raised were matters relating to the permanency of the gifts manifested in the earliest days of the Christian church. No reader of the New Testament could deny that speaking in tongues was common. But was it normative? Did the apostle Paul envision such manifestations of the Spirit's power as being an ongoing feature of the Christian community, or were they restricted to those earliest days? The committee said that "no sure conclusion can be drawn from [Paul's] words as to the normalcy of the continuance or recurrence of any particular charisma in the church beyond the apostolic era" (*Agenda* 1973, p. 421). But neither could such future manifestations be ruled out. Each manifestation of the Spirit required the testing of the Spirit, in consultation with Paul's advice on how to recognize true workings of God.

On the matter of speaking in tongues—arguably one of the most significant manifestations of the Neo-Pentecostal movement—the report was at once wise and pastoral. Although admitting that a person could be psychologically worked up into an ecstatic utterance that resembled glossolalia— and although warning against attempts to "coach" people so as to "get the gift going"—the report concluded that many people genuinely experience this manifestation and gift of the Spirit, and when they do, they must receive it "in thanksgiving and [then] practice it both in love and according to biblical regulations" (*Agenda* 1973, p. 450).

However, the report rejected the teaching—common among some in the charismatic movement—that speaking in tongues was the key indication that a person had been "baptized in the Spirit." First, the report noted that there is no biblical warrant to believe in a Spirit baptism as a separate event from how every believer (at whatever age he or she is baptized) receives the Spirit in the course of baptism into the triune name of God. Second, the report also asserted that glossolalia is just one of many indications that a person has been "filled by the Spirit" and should not, therefore, be construed as the only such indicator (much less as some kind of superior presence of the Spirit over against those who do not evidence the gift).

The "spirit" of the study committee's report on the Spirit can perhaps best be captured in this paragraph—words that display Christian solidarity with and encouragement toward even those with whom Reformed people sometimes disagree:

> Although not in agreement with the Pentecostal and Neo-Pentecostal teaching on the Baptism in the Spirit, we like to state emphatically that every Christian should take seriously the work of the Holy Spirit. We are challenged to discover anew the meaning of the Spirit's work in the believer and the church. We gratefully acknowledge that the Pentecostals have focused attention on the Spirit, whose work has all too often been overlooked or ignored by the established churches. No renewal is really possible without acknowledging the Spirit: his nature, promises, action, and gifts. We may not cease to recognize and pray for God's great gift, the Holy Spirit.
>
> —*Agenda* 1973, p. 438

In the end, the study committee was largely unified in making a series of recommendations to the synod, although committee chairman Bassam Madany did submit a minority report that urged synod to take a stronger stand, declaring Neo-Pentecostal teachings to be unbiblical in stronger terms than the majority of the committee had deemed necessary. Synod, however, adopted the pastoral advice and the specific recommendations as presented by the study committee's majority report. After devoting an entire morning to a thorough examination of and debate on the report, delegates adopted forty discrete pieces of pastoral advice that came out of the massive report. Christian Reformed congregations that were tending in the direction of adopting Neo-Pentecostalist teachings and ideas on baptism and the gifts of the Spirit were directed to bring their teachings back into line with traditional Reformed exegetical insights as reflected in the report.

Also among the recommendations were cautions against delegat-
ing to the annual meeting of synod
those who adhered to the idea of a
"second blessing" or a separate baptism of the Holy Spirit. Although the
overall tone of the report was pastoral and loving, nonetheless Synod
1973 was firm in its stance that those
who urged people to be rebaptized
or who had themselves been rebaptized so as to receive "more" of the
Spirit than they had in their original
baptisms were worthy of stern
counsel and even the discipline of
the church where necessary.
Although seemingly a harsh
response to such matters, the adopt-

Bassam Madany, chair of the study
committee on Neo-Pentecostalism

ed recommendations suggesting discipline were aimed at preserving the
unity of the church at a time when passions had, flared in divisive ways over
precisely these issues.

In the three-and-a-half decades since the 1973 report on Neo-
Pentecostalism, many have returned to this study over and again as one of
the more thoughtful, thorough, and pastoral statements produced on this
topic. Again, however, this significant piece of work was just one part of
Synod 1973. In any given year, a 100+ page report would be more than
enough for the delegates to digest. That year, however, another highly sensitive subject was also before the synod: the issue of homosexuality.

## Homosexuality and the Church

In these early years of the twenty-first century, issues surrounding gay marriage and the rights of homosexual persons have become a reality that all people confront. The issue of the church's attitude toward and treatment of homosexual persons was first brought before synod in 1970 through an overture
brought by the Council of Christian Reformed Churches in Canada. By 2005
Canada had legalized gay marriage. But already in the 1960s the Canadian
government was reexamining its laws and policies toward homosexuals. This

societal shift in attitudes forced the churches in Canada likewise to confront the issue in ways it had not previously done. So Synod 1970 appointed a committee of skilled theologians and respected pastors to look into these matters: chairperson Ralph Heynen, secretary Clarence Boomsma, and Robert Baker, Melvin Hugen, Hudson Nyenhuis, and Henry Stob.

With any sensitive issue, stereotypical thinking, caricatures, and gross misunderstandings are common. Remarkably, the 1973 report nimbly avoided falling into any one of a number of preconceived ideas regarding homosexuality (at least some of which are still common even in 2007). Early in the report committee members stated what was to become their guiding principle: "An important distinction that must be made is the difference between homosexuality as a condition of personal identity and homosexualism as explicit homosexual behavior" (*Agenda* 1973, p. 612).

The report went on to say that although it is by no means clear why some people awaken to having an attraction to people of the same gender, this orientation is not one that a given person decides to have; furthermore, this attraction covers the entire range of human personality and emotion for those who are homosexual. In short, a same-gender attraction goes well beyond the physical alone.

Recognizing this, the report pastorally noted what it called "the plight of the homosexual," detailing the pain that homosexual persons had endured throughout history as they received societal disapproval and judgment—a scorn that many dealt with by choosing to live a lie by outwardly and publicly denying what they inwardly and privately knew to be the truth. Those in the twenty-first century who wish to have homosexuality acknowledged as just one legitimate sexual option among many may not take kindly to the report's labeling of homosexuality as "a problem" or a "condition" with which people had to live and against which they had to struggle. Nevertheless, the report displayed far more compassion and empathy than some might have expected to emerge from a small, somewhat sheltered denomination in the early 1970s.

The report surveyed three Old Testament passages (Gen. 1-2; Gen. 19; Lev. 18-20) and three New Testament passages (1 Cor. 6; 1 Tim. 1:10; Rom. 1). The relatively few number of passages discussed in the report itself bears witness to the common observation that although the writers of the Bible may have assumed a certain attitude toward human sexuality (and specifically toward homosexuality), the fact is that the Bible does not address questions surrounding homosexuality very often or in a systematic way. The committee itself admitted that it is at best difficult to know how normative certain, especially Old Testament, passages are intended to be for today, given that Scripture itself nowhere distinguishes between having a homosexual orientation and engaging in homosexual practices. Even so, the report concluded that the Old Testament forbids homosexual acts and that, insofar as it addresses the issue at all, the New Testament is "in harmony with the Old Testament: homosexual acts are sinful" (*Agenda* 1973, p. 621).

Significantly, in light of new, more contemporary understandings of those who have a same-sex orientation, the report did not label being a homosexual as sinful. It did, however, conclude that same-sex attraction, though not chosen by the one who feels such desires, was nevertheless an example of a fallen created order. Homosexuality represented "a disordered constitution" (*Agenda* 1973, p. 625). The report was quick to note that we all bear the marks of having been born into a fallen world and that those who are gay "need not be considered lesser persons in . . . the church or the kingdom of God" (p. 625). Indeed, affirming homosexuals as persons worthy of love, compassion, respect, and full inclusion in the community of faith was clearly a key goal of the study committee.

For those homosexual persons unable to "reorient" their desires toward persons of the opposite gender, living a life of celibacy and refraining from physical expressions of homosexuality was the recommended, albeit highly difficult, advice the committee gave to the churches and its homosexual members. But the committee did not stop with words directed only to gay persons. Their report went on to urge pastors, officebearers, and congregations to move beyond misunderstandings and stereotypes so as to come to a more accurate understanding of those who struggle with their sexual identity. Only in this way could the church be in a position to offer compassionate, loving support to those in their fellowship who, if they receive only condemnation and stinging misapprehensions within the church community, could very well turn away from the church and become immersed instead in alternative communities where they would not receive the love and hope (and correction) offered by the gospel.

Moreover, homosexual members of the church who endeavored to lead celibate lives were to be included in the life of the church and given the same opportunities as everyone else to exercise their own spiritual gifts, including in providing leadership to a congregation if that is where their gifts led them.

In this area, as in so many others, ignorance fosters only intolerance and leads to rejection, hurt, and anger. The pastoral advice provided in the 1973 report was, therefore, perceived to be its singular contribution to the church's wider discussion of a sensitive subject.

The report's recommendations and pastoral advice were adopted by Synod 1973. In the years that followed, however, many alleged that the CRC had failed significantly to live up to its own rhetoric in providing loving, open support to its homosexual members. By 1996 the issue was once again before the synod when the "Committee to Give Direction about and for Pastoral Care for Homosexual Members" was created and mandated to assess how well (or how poorly) the CRCNA had done in carrying out the recommendations of 1973.

The committee presented its initial findings to Synod 1999. Melvin Hugen, Professor of Pastoral Care at Calvin Theological Seminary, was the only member from the original 1973 study committee to participate in this new study. In surveying congregations throughout the denomination, the committee discovered that not only had most of the 1973 pastoral advice not been carried out very effectively, as a matter of fact there was a significant amount of ignorance among the churches as to the very content of the denomination's official stand on this issue. In response to these findings, the committee recommended a program of education for congregations across the denomination and suggested a "prayer of repentance" for mutual failures in reaching out to those who experience same-sex attraction. After giving the churches a couple of years to consider these matters anew, the committee was to return to Synod 2002 with a final report.

Although generally in agreement with the original study, the 2002 report urged even greater care in how the church and its individual members speak of homosexual persons so as to avoid injurious labeling (which could lead to further stereotyping). The report also deepened what in 1973 had been labeled the "plight" of persons experiencing same-sex attractions by reminding the denomination of the great shame and confusion frequently experienced by members within the church's fellowship who struggle with sexual identity. In particular, the report attempted to heighten sensitivity toward—and remind CRC members of the need to be gracious with—those who find the leading of a celibate life to be difficult and fraught with temptations and failures. Rather than treat celibacy and all it entails as something that is easy to recommend and equally easy to carry out, it is the church's responsibility to recognize the difficulties inherent in this and so to encourage the gifts of celibacy and self-control, nurturing especially those who struggle. Ultimately the 2002 report presented detailed advice for how to set up effective pastoral ministries to persons with same-sex attractions, including two detailed Appendices with recommended readings, models for ministry, and resource persons as well as summaries of current biological and psychological perspectives relating to these issues.

Synod 2002 adopted these new recommendations and commended them to the churches for study, review, and implementation. How well such advice is being carried out remains a source of discussion, even as some in the wider world have long since derided what remains the CRCNA's core stance of embracing the homosexual person while still condemning and rejecting homosexual behaviors and lifestyles. However, even as in the early years of the twenty-first century synod was refining its pastoral advice for

Mel Hugen, a member of both study committees on homosexuality

effective and compassionate ministries, issues related to homosexuality were already getting framed in new ways. Some began to suggest that perhaps in addition to the option of celibacy, the church needs to recognize the validity of lifelong, monogamous gay relationships or unions. Some writers, including respected CRC thinkers like the late Lewis B. Smedes, suggested that even as we accept, albeit perhaps with regret, the presence of divorced and remarried persons within the church's fellowship and leadership, perhaps a way could be found to accept also those who display commitment and faithfulness (and who reject promiscuous lifestyles) by remaining true to one partner in a homosexual union.

By 2004 and 2005, synod had begun to deal with this new aspect of the wider debate when First CRC (Toronto) indicated it was exploring the option of allowing people in such committed gay relationships to serve as elders and deacons within their congregation. In addressing this matter, synod continued to uphold the 1973 recommendations that rule out acceptance of such unions. But even as the Canadian government in 2005 sanctioned same-sex marriages, so individual states in the United States were likewise experimenting with legislation to accomplish the same thing. As the CRCNA looks into the near-term future, it seems clear that neither 1973 nor 2002 have provided the last opportunity to ponder this vital and often painful matter.

## Ordination: What and for Whom?

Finally, our survey of Synod 1973 must include a summary of another large report from a study committee appointed in 1969 on the nature of the ordained offices in the church. The study committee, headed by John Primus and with Anthony Hoekema serving as the report's author, had originally submitted its work to Synod 1972, only to have synod return the report to them for further refinement and elaboration. Synod 1973 accepted the revised report and the delegates adopted all of its recommendations. The immediate rationale for studying this issue centered on a desire to understand the nature of nonordained laypersons in the church as well as the role and function of evangelists. In the end the study committee concluded, in good Reformed fashion, that it is wholly appropriate to see every believer in Christ's church as sharing a common vocation of *diakonia* or service. Every believer is in a sense called to advance the kingdom by witnessing to the reality of Christ Jesus as Lord and Savior of all.

However, biblical warrant and vast historical precedent suggest the need to set aside specific individuals within the church who are able to devote themselves more fully to certain necessary tasks such as preaching, administering the sacraments, engaging in mission work, and other specialized tasks. Ordination implies no elevation of pastors, elders, and deacons over the rest of the congregation but recognizes a certain "setting aside" of individuals who are clearly called to a specific task and who have been consequently gifted by God's Spirit to carry out that task.

In addition to significant biblical and historical summaries, the study committee dealt at some length with questions as to the "authority" inherent in those who are set aside in the ordained offices of the church. The final report noted that in a sense, humanity as created in the image of God had been given a form of authorization from the very beginning to be God's special representatives in this world. Both the man and the woman in Eden were authorized by God to carry out God's work on God's behalf (and in a manner, one assumes, consistent with how God himself would carry it out). Within the church, all authority stems from Christ Jesus alone, who is the head of the church. As Jesus gave authority to his original disciples-turned-apostles, so he continues to authorize ongoing kingdom work through the gift of the Holy Spirit until he comes again. In the words of the report, "the church, therefore, is neither a hierarchy nor an aristocracy, oligarchy, or democracy. It is rather a 'Christ-ruled brotherhood'" (*Agenda* 1973, p. 693).

In general, the study committee asserted that Christ's authority must not be construed as a dominating power exercised by the few over the many in any manner that would suggest hierarchy. The authority of Christ is the authority of the one who came to serve, not to be served, to lay his life down for many, not to laud his life or his power over anyone. "The special ministries do not stand above the congregation in the place of Christ, nor does the congregation stand above the special ministries in the place of Christ. Both stand beneath the authority of Christ" (*Agenda* 1973, p. 709).

In reminding the denomination that the fundamental authority of Jesus is loving service in order to display the good news of Jesus' grace, the study committee nowhere addressed the question of whether such service-oriented authority is restricted to males or whether females could be "set aside" in ordained service as well. But already in 1973 exactly that question was being asked in ever more serious and earnest ways. Over the next twenty-two sessions of synod this question would occupy center stage in a kind of theological and ecclesiastical see-saw that at times appeared never-ending.

# WOMEN IN OFFICE

Scientists tell us that the way a question is phrased can have a significant impact on the answer. After a quarter-century of denominational work on the question of whether or not women are allowed to serve in the ordained offices of the church, Synod 1995 said something similar about the biblical witness in this matter. That is, if you frame the question based on the premise that women are not allowed to be ministers or elders, the Bible may reveal to you an answer that affirms this prohibition. On the other hand, if you frame the question with the idea that women may be able to serve in these offices, you may find an answer that opens the door to that possibility. Of course the Bible cannot say two contradictory things on this or any other vital question. Hence synod never said that the Bible teaches two conflicting, opposite ideas on the question of women in office—only that it was possible for people wielding the same rock-solid, Reformed hermeneutical tools of interpretation on the same biblical texts to come to opposite conclusions.

In other words, synod was not able to say definitively which viewpoint was right. At the same time, it declared that we cannot easily call either side wrong. Depending on your point of view, the 1995 solution to this long-running debate was either a Solomon-like stroke of wisdom or a ridiculous straddling of a biblical fence (and it has in various ways been called both). There was something unprecedented about claiming that thoughtful, intelligent people of goodwill could wield the very best of interpretive tools and yet still arrive at divergent conclusions. What could account for such a novel stance? Perhaps the answer lies in over twenty synods' worth of debate.

Those who followed the so-called "women in office debate" in the CRC know what a roller coaster ride it was. Many key decisions were made with such a thin majority one way or the other that with just a slight change in the configuration of synodical delegates in a given year, what had been decided one year could well be reversed the very next year. Since several of the key points of dispute involved a change in the Church Order—and since Church Order changes mandated a two-year process in which any change synod made had to be ratified by the next synod—the synodical boat constantly rocked from one side to the other. For instance, one synod would declare that women could serve as deacons, after which many congregations would elect female deacons the first chance they got. But then the next synod would declare that women could not so serve the church, and congregations with female deacons would be told to remove them from office as soon as possible.

Driving this synodical back-and-forth movement were passions that ran deep on all sides. Few, if any, approached this question casually. Few, if any, claimed that what the Bible had to say in this regard was irrelevant. Instead, intense scholarship of the highest caliber and seriousness of purpose lay behind every study report the synod received, and no small amount of prayer and theological thoughtfulness fueled the scores of overtures synod received over the years. It was precisely this high level of study that led synod finally to conclude that for the foreseeable future, simply applying our minds to the matter would not end the dispute. Indeed, the prudent application of fine minds consistently yielded opposite results. No one was making mistakes. No one appeared to be taking interpretive shortcuts. And yet . . .

Even summarizing the bevy of study reports and overtures synod received from the early 1970s through the late 1990s is a daunting task. As indicated earlier in this volume, however, Synod 1973, which received an eighty-page report (commissioned by Synod 1970) on the question of women serving in the offices of the church is as good a place to begin this saga as any. In what would turn out to be a good example of dramatic understatement, synod that year decided to defer action and refer the report to the churches for reaction because "the importance of this subject demands that we proceed with care" (*Acts* 1973, p. 86).

It is perhaps no surprise that Synod 1973 blinked a bit when confronted with the report. The study committee, chaired by Remkes Kooistra, not only delivered a lengthy and well-written report, it proffered conclusions that must have been nothing short of startling to many of the delegates. The report asked synod to adopt the statement that "the practice of excluding women from ecclesiastical office cannot conclusively be defended on biblical grounds." It stated further that redemption in Christ should disallow "any discrimination in the congregation," which is perhaps why "during the times of biblical history women have in fact officiated in many ways and in many offices" (p. 588). The committee also called for further study of this issue, including "whether the word 'male' in Article 3 of the Church Order should be deleted" (*Acts* 1973, p. 588).

Remkes Kooistra, chair of the 1973 study committee on women in office

Synod did indeed decide to study the matter, asking for a report not later than 1975. But beyond the ins and outs of what would in the end be a large pile of study committee reports, what Synod 1973 unleashed was one of the longest-running debates in CRC history. Synodical meetings in future years would become media events filmed by local television stations, written about in national magazines and newspapers, and attended by standing-room-only crowds of onlookers who alternately cheered and wept over the many votes that would be taken. Periodicals such as *The Banner, The Reformed*

*Journal,* and *Outlook* became forums for numerous articles written by pastors, seminary professors, and church members alike, even as whole new journals were founded to discuss only this towering issue.

Not a few CRCNA members found this entire matter to be unsettling in a foundational way. By the time of the denomination's sesquicentennial, it will have been a dozen years since the 1995 decision that opened the door to female pastors and elders (albeit by way of a local option). The issue was revisited in 2000 and again in 2005, and although certain restrictions remain in place, the local option to ordain women into all the offices of the church remained in place.

What we may forget in 2007, however, is that it was a scant fifty years earlier, during the centennial year of 1957, that the CRC first granted women the right to vote in congregational meetings. Even this was its own kind of local option—as late as 1972 synod still refused to *require* congregations to give women the right to vote. Yet somehow, in the sixteen years between 1957 and 1973, some folks were talking about letting women go well beyond voting yes or no on the annual church budget—they were saying that women should be allowed to preach God's Word from CRC pulpits. This shift occurred so quickly that many became convinced that the CRC was losing its moorings in the Bible in favor of letting secular society (and the wider women's rights and equal opportunity movements) trump the witness of Scripture.

But as future years would make clear, even if the church agreed to restrict its focus to the biblical revelation, this issue of women in office was far from easily settled. Indeed, in 1975 the committee that had been asked to review the 1973 report and receive reactions to it presented its report. The committee had received 165 communications (mostly negative reactions), leading them to conclude that it would be highly divisive and hence inadvisable to open the ordained offices of the church to women at that time. In the course of presenting their report to Synod 1975, this review committee mentioned that among the stumbling blocks to granting a woman authority in the church was figuring out how to reconcile that status with a woman being under the authority of her husband as head of the household. Could a woman be in authority over men in the church when on the home front she was under the authority of a man?

Thus suddenly the issue of "headship" was brought to synod. In some ways this was the next logical step in the wider discussion about women in office. After all, if women were under the authority of men as part of God's original created order, then the dimensions of this entire debate would shift significantly. If that were the case, then clearly nothing in the New Testament or its words about authority in Christ's church could challenge or displace that creation ordinance. But in addition to raising this aspect of the wider discussion, Synod 1975 urged congregations to make full use of women's gifts in the church, albeit within the Church Order strictures barring them from ordained office. It also called for a new committee to study nothing less than the whole sweep of Scripture, both the Old and the New Testaments, to determine a proper interpretive approach to the key texts concerning a woman's role and place in the church.

This new study committee's mandate was daunting. Called "The Committee on Hermeneutical Principles Concerning Women in Ecclesiastical Office," the group included scholars such as Andrew Bandstra, Marten Woudstra, Paul Bremer, David Engelhard, Sidney Greidanus, and Simon Kistemaker. Their report, submitted to Synod 1978, laid out the terms and definitions of a Reformed approach to biblical interpretation and then used this framework to approach and comment on key Old and New Testament passages including Genesis 1-3, Galatians 3:28, various passages in 1 Corinthians, and the key passage of 1 Timothy 2.

In the end, the report said that there does appear to be a principle of headship of the man over the woman in marriage. Further, this authority of the man over the woman may not be a result of humanity's fall into sin but may have been part of the created order, and therefore this needed to be upheld not only in marriage but also in the church. The New Testament, however, displays the equal worth of both men and women, and there can be no denying that the Spirit's gifts for service in the church are for people of both genders. The report also asserted that whereas the New Testament clearly shows that women have a role to play in the community of Christ's church, "no biblical passage speaks directly to the question of women in ecclesiastical office as presently understood" (*Agenda* 1978, p. 529).

The committee was able to agree on most of these broad ideas but diverged on what specific action to recommend. Although they appear to have agreed to make some kind of recommendation to allow women to serve as deacons, the question became how to frame such a suggestion. Four of the committee's six members recommended that the office of deacon be opened to women based on biblical and historical evidence for allowing this, and that consistories in all churches should be given the right to so ordain women. Two of the members, however, put in a qualifying line that women could be ordained as deacons "provided that their work is distinguished from that of elders" (*Agenda* 1978, p. 532). When these recommendations were brought to the floor on June 21, 1978, the majority recommendation was defeated in favor of passing the minority report, which included the qualification.

Although this decision looked to be a step in the right direction for those who favored the full use of women's gifts, the fact is that the decision caused some unhappiness on all sides. Certainly those who opposed the ordination of women to any office had cause for alarm, as this appeared to be a prelude to all that they did not wish to see happen in their beloved denomination. But even those on the other side of the question perceived some troubling features to the 1978 decision. First, some found the report's view on the headship of men over women questionable, particularly its implication that headship extended beyond marriage to the church. Second, the decision of Synod 1978 apparently allowed a downgrading of the office of deacon.

Traditionally, the offices of minister, elder, and deacon had all been perceived as having equal status as ordained offices through which qualified persons could serve the church. By contrast, in order to maintain the idea of male headship, the office of deacon was now being viewed as having little or no authority; instead it was seen as a service-based office (as opposed to the offices of minister and elder, which were still viewed as having a kind of authority that the office of deacon lacked).

By the following year, however, opinions on the 1978 decision were rendered moot. According to Church Order, the change approved by Synod 1978 had to be ratified by Synod 1979—a step that synod refused to take. Sixty-four overtures and communications poured into the Agenda for Synod 1979, most asking for further study on the questions that had been raised (but not answered) by the 1978 report. Not surprisingly, a fourth major study committee was commissioned. Meanwhile, churches that had elected women deacons on the assumption that the 1978 decision would be ratified were told that female officebearers could serve out their terms but that until this matter was settled, women must not be nominated for deacon again.

Two years later the situation had not improved. The deeply divided committee that came to Synod 1981 presented not less than three sets of recommendations: one majority report and two minority reports. Perhaps it was a fitting symbol for the divided nature of the church at that time that a committee of eight people divided four, three, and one as to what the church should do. The majority report again recommended that the CRC allow women to be ordained as deacons as long as this work was seen as different from the work of elders and ministers. The first minority report submitted by three committee members addressed confusion over the nature of the church's offices by distinguishing between the "restricted consistory" of just the elders and the pastor and the "board of deacons" made up of only the deacons. Whereas the consistory included pastors, elders, and deacons, only the re-named "restricted consistory" would handle matters that dealt with the actual (authoritative) governance of the congregation. Having made those clarifications, the first minority report recommended allowing the office of deacon to be open to all qualifying members, male and female alike. The second minority recommendation came from

Thea Van Halsema, author of a minority report advocating the creation of a new, non-ordained category of church workers called "assistants in ministry"

one member of the committee who recommended that the prohibition against women in any office of the church be continued.

At every meeting of synod, recommendations and the study committee reports come to delegates by way of various advisory committees who make formal motions for them to consider. In 1981, not only was synod faced with a fractured study committee report, the advisory committee itself could not reach consensus and so brought a majority and a minority set of recommendations before the wider body. On June 16, after an entire morning's worth of spirited debate, there was no resolution in sight. The debate continued all afternoon, again with no progress. The next morning elder delegate George Vander Velde moved that the entire matter, stretching back to 1978, be postponed until such time as another study committee (the fifth such major committee) would come back with further clarification on the matter of male headship. No doubt sensing a way out of what was clearly an impasse, synod adopted this motion.

The fifth lengthy report on these matters did not arrive until Synod 1984. Once again, it included one majority report and two minority reports. In total, the report ran to over ninety tightly packed pages of material, fifty-three of which were the shank of the report, with the remaining pages devoted to minority reports. A minority report submitted by committee member Thea Van Halsema sought to find a third way out of the impasse by creating a non-ordained category of "assistants in ministry" by which women could assist ordained persons in all areas of the church's work but without themselves being in charge of that work. The second minority report was submitted by Willis De Boer and Sarah Cook, who claimed that it is unwarranted biblically to extend male headship in marriage to the life of the church and that, there-fore, all offices of the church should be opened to men and women alike.

But it was the majority report whose recommendations made it to the floor. The minutes of Synod 1984 reveal a tortured, emotional, and exhausting debate that stretched out over two days. Once again, when the ballots were cast and counted, synod had adopted resolutions that unsettled almost everyone. Those advocating the full use of women's gifts in the church were deeply troubled by the study committee's conclusion that "the headship principle, which means that the man should exercise primary leadership and direction-setting in the home and in the church, is a biblical teaching recognized in both the Old and the New Testament." Having debated, tabled, and then re-debated various versions of this assertion, Synod 1984 finally adopted this language as the stance of the CRCNA. When it did so, thirty-two of synod's 160 delegates had their negative responses recorded. Two delegates submitted written protests to be recorded in the minutes, including Leonard Vander Zee, who wrote, "Finding no other way to stop . . . women in office, [synod] has created a new 'principle of headship' which is unbiblical in nature and unworkable in practice . . . This decision binds the consciences of many members in a matter on which the Bible is unclear and the creeds are not at stake" (*Acts* 1984, p. 623).

The next day, however, Synod 1984 returned to the postponed decision of 1978 and, to the surprise of many, voted to reaffirm and simultaneously rati-fy changing the Church Order so as to allow women to be ordained as dea-cons. After this vote, thirty-one delegates recorded their negative votes and thirteen individuals submitted (sometimes lengthy) written comments of protest. Ironically, written protests on both sides of the women-in-office debate claimed that the motion in question lacked biblical warrant and proof. The Bible, interpreted by the best minds in the CRC and always approached with due reverence and holy respect, was being referenced on all sides but without reaching a consensus on definitive biblical answers. Only in the 1990s did synod come to the realization that, as strange as it seems to Bible-believing Christians, this appeared to be an issue that solid biblical scholarship alone was not going to resolve any time soon.

Beyond synod, the debate was carried on in innumerable discussions across Canada and the United States in council, consistory, and classis meetings, in seminary classrooms, and in the pages of CRCNA-related periodicals. The Committee for Women in the Christian Reformed Church distributed information, held seminars, and brought in speakers such as Neal Plantinga to address annual banquets under the banner theme "Partnership in the Gospel." Calvin Theological Seminary professor John W. Cooper distributed a white paper titled "A Cause for Division?" This paper was soon answered by a corresponding pamphlet by Nelson Kloosterman and Cornelis P. Venema, who removed the question mark from Cooper's title as an initial way to state their contention that this was indeed "A Cause of Division." Whereas Cooper and many on the seminary faculty believed that people with solid reverence for Scripture could disagree on this issue, Kloosterman and Venema stated their contention that the belief that women could be ordained into the offices of the church required a disrespecting of Scripture and the employing of non-Reformed approaches to God's Word.

Meanwhile writers such as Calvin Seminary professor Neal Plantinga were advancing a position in favor of women in office by way of analogy. In an April 17, 1989, article in *The Banner,* Plantinga pointed out that the New Testament's words about accepting slavery—and even of telling slaves to accept their lot in life as part of their larger obedience to their Lord Jesus—are at least as clear (and maybe more frequent) than whatever the New Testament may have to say about women serving in the offices of the church. Even so, Plantinga said, few contemporary Christians accept the idea that one human being may own another and so interpret biblical texts that promote (or at least accept) slavery in ways that had not been done during other periods of history. Plantinga believed that the gospel's intent was to return us to all that we were created to be—an intent that continues to unfold before us as the Holy Spirit leads us into all truth. Accepting women in church leadership positions can be done in the same way (and by the same principle) by

John Cooper

Nelson Kloosterman

which slavery is now rejected. "The full partnership of women with men, like the full redemption of slaves, is not a secular novelty but a deeply Christian one. . . . Slave subordination and female subordination are in the same hermeneutical boat; often they are in the same passage. They are both part of a bad dream from the old world, gradually overcome by the mission of Jesus" (*The Banner,* 4/17/89, p. 14).

In that same issue of *The Banner* Cornelis P. Venema presented the case for preserving the tradition of male-only clergy and elders. Venema did not see the move toward change as an example of the unfolding of redemption as Plantinga did. Instead he asserted that the CRC was on the verge of allowing the winds of societal fashion to usurp the authority of Scripture. For Venema, the Bible is clear and persuasive on this question. "Will the Bible have the first and last word in our churches . . . ? The women-in-office issue tests our resolve to pattern our lives as men and women, in the home and church, after the pattern of the Lord's Word" (p. 17).

As people everywhere continued to debate these issues, the delegates to Synod 1990 accomplished something many had begun to suspect was impossible regarding this issue: they surprised everyone! Synod that year had received the sixth major report on issues related to women in office.

Commissioned in 1987, the four-member study committee in 1990 presented the first united report in many years. The committee questioned the validity of the 1984 decision to extend the headship principle to all areas of church, life, and society, and raised biblical reasons for doubting the truth of this idea. But it was the advisory committee that processed this report for the delegates that provided the real surprise: a majority of its members recommended to synod that this entire matter be left up to local congregations. Startlingly, the committee suggested opening *all* the church's offices to women. After eight hours of debate, the motion passed 99-84. People on both sides of the debate seemed genuinely stunned. "What just happened here?" was a frequently-asked question among the hundreds of people who came to witness the discussion and vote. When the dust had settled, those who had long advocated for the full use of women's gifts were jubilant. Those on the other side were deeply saddened and troubled.

Neal Plantinga

Spectators at Synod 1990 react to the debate on women in office

In the four years that followed, people on both sides of the issue found themselves changing roles every other year: those who had been happy one year were disappointed the next, and vice-versa. Synod 1992 reversed Synod 1990. Women were once again barred from the offices of minister and elder. Synod 1993 reversed Synod 1992 and recommended a return to the 1990 decision to open all the offices by way of a local option. Synod 1994 reversed Synod 1993 by failing to ratify the change in the Church Order proposed at the prior synod. As James Schaap characterized it, synod had become a never-ending badminton match with the women-in-office issue serving as the shuttlecock that was now on this side of the net, then on the other.

Synod 1995 decided to end all these back-and-forth reversals. A quarter-century after Synod 1970 had begun the current discussion, delegates arriving in Grand Rapids in June 1995 were again besieged. The section of the agenda devoted to overtures and communications ran to 230 pages. The vast majority of the eighty overtures and nine communications were about women in office. Although there was no major report on the issue that year, synod had to find a way to address the avalanche of overtures coming from all sides.

The delegates were asked to vote on a motion that would not change the Church Order (and that would not, therefore, require ratification the following year) but that would alter the sense of Church Order Article 3 so as to permit a local option: "A classis may, in response to local needs and circumstances, declare that the word *male* in Article 3-a of the Church Order is inoperative and may authorize the churches under its jurisdiction to ordain and install women in the offices of elder, minister, and evangelist."

Synod considered a further motion to suspend debate on this issue until 2000, when it would be reviewed. As noted at the outset of this chapter, the grounds given were that it had become clear over the years that through the good exercise of the same exegetical and hermeneutical tools, Christian brothers and sisters of good will could—and regularly did—arrive at opposing conclusions. The majority recommendation of the advisory committee put it this way: "Synod recognize[s] that there are two different perspectives and convictions, both of which honor the Scriptures as the infallible Word of God, on the issue whether women are allowed to serve in the offices of elder, minister, and evangelist" (*Acts* 1995, p. 731). In the afternoon session of Monday, June 19, 1995, this motion was adopted. That evening, after vigorous debate, the committee's main recommendation to grant classes a local option was also adopted. Twenty delegates registered their negative votes into the record, eight of which included brief written protests. But the matter had passed.

Next was a series of eight further strictures, which included prohibitions on women being delegated to synod as well as guidelines on the future presentation of female candidates for the ministry. Procedures were approved to protect the consciences of those who disapprove of women serving as pastors.

In the years that followed, particularly the next year at Synod 1996, attempts were made to reverse the decision of 1995. But the five-year moratorium held and no significant votes were taken on the matter again until 2000. At that time a review was held as to how the 1995 decision had been accepted and implemented. There were some attempts to dismantle 1995, even as others tried to maintain the local option but loosen up some of the

other strictures that still limited a woman's role in the denomination, its agencies, and its ministries. But synod decided to leave the matter where it was and mandated a similar review in 2005. That synod again received requests to reduce or eliminate the remaining restrictions, but decided that until a majority of the CRCNA's forty-seven classes had approved women as ministers, elders, and evangelists, the bulk of the 1995 restrictions would remain in place for the sake of preserving the unity that had been achieved since 1995.

In 2005, 46 percent of the denomination's classes had approved allowing women to serve in all the offices. The study committee that

In 1996, Ruth Hofman was the first woman ordained to preaching ministry in the CRC

reported to Synod 2005 presented the results of a large survey of the CRCNA. When asked how the 1995 decision had affected congregations and classes, most reported that the decision had not significantly changed matters for good or for ill. Two-thirds of the congregations responding said that this decision had had a mixed effect or no effect at all; just 18 percent claimed it had had a negative effect on their congregation and its attitude toward the wider denomination. Similar results showed up across the survey's multiple questions.

As of May 2006, the denomination had passed the halfway mark: 25 classes (53 percent) had approved allowing women to serve in all offices of the church.

When the Christian Reformed Church in North America turned 100 years old in 1957, women were granted the right to vote in congregational meetings. A dozen or so years later, when the denomination began to consider the question of women serving in all the offices, some congregations had not yet given their female members this option. As the denomination now turns 150, women are allowed to serve in all the offices of the church in more than half of the denomination's classes and congregations. Although still a small fraction of the overall number of pastors in the CRCNA, each year more women are entering the ordained ministry as pastors. But considering what a dramatic change that represents since 1957, it is perhaps no surprise that many still feel pain over this issue, even as others express a degree of confusion and consternation that the denomination arrived at the point it did in 1995 and beyond.

Of course, it is also painfully true that the denomination as a whole suffered as a result of those long years of turmoil and never-ending debate. In 1992 overall membership in the CRCNA hit an all-time high of just over 316,000 members across 981 congregations. In the 1980s Christian Reformed Home Missions had optimistically adopted the mission slogan "400,000 by 2000," indicating a desire to see the denomination grow to 400,000 members by the turn of the millennium. Athough some in the denomination objected to setting such a numeric marker for mission success, the goal was actually a modest one, representing just 2 percent growth across a fifteen-year span.

But by 2000, despite successful efforts at new church planting and steady growth through evangelism efforts, the denomination had suffered a net loss of just over 40,000 members. Those numbers alone cannot tell the stories of pain and division as a number of congregations split apart and seceded from the Christian Reformed Church. Here and there were reports of bitter disputes over church property and assets; even of families who were divided among themselves. But the exit from the CRC was not limited to those who disagreed with the decision allowing women to serve. Many others left the denomination out of frustration over its lack of conviction and progress in allowing women to serve fully. Clearly, this was an issue capable of generating strong reactions on both ends of the spectrum.

In an important sense, the 1995 decision may have been a brilliant and wise solution to an intractable problem that was sapping the denomination of energy, vitality, and holy joy. Over time, some who have been blessed by the ministry of women pastors and elders have testified that their minds were changed by seeing what could only be the Holy Spirit at work in the ministry of these ordained women. Still others have reported that it was only when their own daughters or granddaughters received a clear call from the Lord that they realized that perhaps the Lord was doing a new work in ways that proved traditional interpretations of certain texts wrong.

Ultimately, the 1995 decision called on all members of the church to honor and respect the integrity and commitment to God's Word of those who continue to be persuaded that this is the wrong way to go. In a 1989 editorial, then-*Banner* editor Andrew Kuyvenhoven wrote, "In no way should we allow our differences on this issue to drive us apart. We need each other. Let us study, pray, and exchange insights. . . . If we continue to look to God, God will see us through" (April 17, p. 7).

As we celebrate our sesquicentennial theme of "Grace through every generation," we can be grateful to God that although the CRCNA weathered a painfully difficult time in this last half-century of our life together, God's grace has somehow seen us through, and will stick with us in all the years ahead too. "We need each other," Kuyvenhoven rightly said. Thanks be to God that across our differences, we still have each other too.

*Chapter Five*

# THE GROWING FAMILY

A s we've already noted, around the time the Christian Reformed Church celebrated its hundredth birthday, Christian Reformed congregations across North America were fairly similar. Visitors to any CRC could be fairly certain of what to expect: certain commonalities of language, worship style, music, and sermon delivery were, if not uniform exactly, pretty much the same all over. In 2007 the situation is vastly different. Over the past fifty years the CRCNA has experienced significant changes, most of which correlate closely with larger ecclesiastical, sociological, and cultural changes on the North American scene. The result is that the CRCNA at 150 years old looks very different from the denomination that existed only a half-century ago. In this chapter and the next we will explore two key areas of change: the growing ethnic diversity within the CRC and the ever-increasing liturgical diversity that characterizes many congregations within the larger denomination.

Immigrants arriving from the Netherlands

It's worth noting that at the same time the CRCNA was celebrating its centennial in 1957, the United States in particular was on the cusp of undergoing a shift in immigration patterns. The United States, of course, had long been perceived as a land of opportunity by peoples from around the world. But prior to the mid-twentieth century, the vast majority of immigrants came from Europe. Indeed, the CRC itself came into being and then grew substantially through the influx of Dutch immigrants in the nineteenth century. Earlier we noted that the explosion of church growth in Canada likewise resulted from a post-World War II boom in Dutch immigration through the ports of Halifax and Montreal; a pattern of European immigration that reflects the overall situation in North America throughout the nineteenth century and right up to the middle of the twentieth.

By 1960, however, the situation had changed as immigration from Europe slowed considerably even as immigration from Asia, Central and South America, and Mexico burgeoned. In 1965 the U.S. Congress lifted its former immigration quota system, thus further opening the immigration floodgates to people from around the world. Not surprisingly, the majority of immigrants who arrived in North America after the 1950s journeyed from home countries that were bursting at the seams, often with rising levels of poverty and overcrowded urban centers. Overall, immigration to the United States continued to rise. From 1981-1990 a total of 7.3 million people formally immigrated to the United States; an additional 9.1 million arrived during the next decade. Similarly, in Canada immigration swelled from around 500,000 persons per year in the 1950s to nearly 2.25 million per year in 2000. But more significant to note than the number of immigrants are the countries of origin of the vast majority of these new citizens.

During the 1950s when the CRCNA turned 100, immigration from places like Mexico, Korea, and the rest of Asia was very modest. From 1951-1960, for example, immigrants from Asia numbered approximately 150,000; by the 1990s that number had swelled to 2.8 million. Similarly Korean immigrants to the U.S. during the 1950s numbered just over 6,000. However, from 1970-2000 Korean immigrants numbered close to a quarter million people each decade. Immigration from Mexico increased from just shy of 300,000 people during the 1950s to 2.3 million during the 1990s. Given the population growth in many Asian and Latin American nations, this influx is not surprising. There are now over 25 cities worldwide with populations in excess of 10 million people. Population densities per square mile in some cities now reach staggering numbers in excess of 150,000 people. Mexico City is home to 22.7 million citizens. India alone has three cities of more than 15 million people each: Bombay is home to 19.7 million, New Delhi another 19.5 million, and Calcutta now counts nearly 16 million residents.

Ministry with Cuban immigrants in North Haledon, New Jersey

Even as this latest wave of immigration has changed the overall face of North American society, so it has changed the complexion of many denominations, including the CRCNA. Not surprisingly, Christian Reformed Home Missions has led the way in diversifying the CRC in ways that now help the denomination reflect more fully the broad spectrum of God's people around

Ramon Borrego

the world. Under the banner "Gathering God's Growing Family," Home Missions has planted churches and raised up new leaders in ways that have significantly changed the face of the denomination.

Indeed, in 2007 the CRCNA includes two classes comprised primarily of specific non-Anglo ethnic groups. Classis Red Mesa, formed in 1982, was the tangible culmination of the earliest mission effort of the CRC (begun in 1896) among the Navajo and Zuni people in New Mexico and Arizona. Classis Red Mesa now includes seventeen organized or emerging congregations that are home to nearly 2,000 members.

By 1996 Korean immigration, especially to California, had grown sufficiently that Classis Pacific Hanmi was formed. The twenty-three organized or emerging congregations in this classis now include 1,500 CRC members. Recent membership trends indicate that the growth of this classis and its member congregations continues to increase steadily as now second and even third generations of Korean-Americans establish themselves along the West Coast.

But those statistics hardly tell the larger, richer story. As noted above, the CRCNA's centennial celebration coincided with major immigration and population shifts in both the United States and Canada. At almost the same time, increasing numbers of Christian Reformed pastors and mission workers were likewise awakening to new opportunities for growth and outreach. Beginning in the 1940s, through the pioneering work of missionary Bessie

VanderValk from Paterson, New Jersey, the CRC had begun to establish a mission presence in Cuba. VanderValk's work went sufficiently well that by the mid-1950s additional missionaries were dispatched to Cuba, including Clarence Nyenhuis and Jerry Pott. By 1960, however, conditions in Cuba changed drastically following the fall of Batista and the rise of Castro. In addition to making mission work in Cuba dangerous, if not impossible, this significant political shift caused a burgeoning of Cuban refugees to begin coming ashore in nearby Florida. Within two years of the Castro takeover, 30,000 Cubans had fled to Florida. As a result, many of the missionaries who had formerly worked in Cuba refocused their efforts on southern Florida, thus establishing a number of the CRCNA's first Hispanic congregations.

Meanwhile, elsewhere across North America, many CRC leaders began to recognize the rich possibilities inherent in reaching out to Hispanic communities. Between 1970 and 1995, the Hispanic population in the United States jumped seventy-five fold. In the midst of this population explosion, Christian Reformed leaders like Alfred Mulder seized the opportunity to establish new congregations specifically aimed at ministering to these sisters and brothers from Mexico, Latin America, and South America. In the mid-1980s people from all denominations awoke to the need for such churches. In California, for example, the ratio of Protestant churches to Hispanic persons was 1:4,294.

To begin making connections with this large population, the CRC began to produce Spanish-language materials and began Spanish broadcasts of the Back to God Hour radio ministry. What was most needed, however, were indigenous leaders for new congregations. To meet this need, Christian Reformed leaders like Ramon Borrego, Gary Teja, and Duane VanderBrug began working with Calvin Theological Seminary and the International Theological Seminary in Los Angeles to establish an on-site Evangelism Training Program. This equipping of new leaders bore much fruit throughout the 1980s and 1990s as many new Spanish-speaking congregations formed in California and also in Florida, New Jersey, and Texas.

As noted already, the surge in Korean immigration to North America also coincided with the past fifty years of CRCNA history. But the loving bonds that eventually were forged between the CRC and the Korean people went beyond the sheer increase in the number of Koreans coming to California and elsewhere.

As early as 1964, when Calvin Theological Seminary President John Kromminga returned from a semester as visiting professor at Hapdong

Seminary in Seoul with high enthusiasm for the Christian fervor he saw among the Korean people, the denomination began taking active steps to cement a relationship with the Korean church. Kromminga's groundbreaking work and subsequent reports to the seminary and synod resulted in a 1965 synodical goal of raising $30,000 for the construction of new facilities at Hapdong Seminary. Exactly forty years later in October 2004, Calvin Seminary President Neal

Myung Suk Lee, first Korean director of Coffee Break Ministries

Plantinga visited Korea and once again made contact with key leaders in the Korean community, including teachers at the seminary. In a further indication of the denomination's influence on the Korean church scene, Plantinga preached at Sarang Community Church, whose pastor, Jung Hyun Oh, is a graduate of Calvin Theological Seminary. Only twenty-five years old, the Sarang church is home to some 30,000 members who worship each Sunday in five different worship services (the first of which begins at 5:30 a.m.!).

Thus began what has proven to be a richly rewarding relationship between Korean Christians and the CRCNA. By the time of Plantinga's trip in the fall of 2004, the Korean presence in the denomination and at the seminary had grown dramatically. In 1983 only seven Koreans or Korean-Americans were enrolled at Calvin Seminary; by 2005 that number had grown to sixty-three students—20 percent of the entire student body. Through the introduction of its Ph.D. program in the 1990s, the seminary is able to train and equip future Korean professors of theology who can instruct the next generation of church leaders in Korea.

Among the early pioneers in helping to grow the Korean part of the CRC are leaders like John E. Kim, Jin Tae Lee, John T. Kim, Paul Yang, and Myung Suk Lee. In the late 1970s John E. Kim and Jin Tae Lee completed their theological education at Calvin Theological Seminary. After graduation, each pastor headed to California to establish new congregations among the Koreans living there. These efforts proved hugely successful: within years of founding new congregations, both Revs. Kim and Lee were overseeing significant ministries that included multimillion-dollar facilities and steadily expanding memberships. Currently some of the Korean congregations in California are among the largest in the denomination, including All Nations Church in Lake Terrace, with a membership of 1,400.

A key component in the growth of Korean congregations is their prayerful spirituality. For many years, the CRC Coffee Break program had been widely successful as a ministry to women. The program appealed also to Korean congregations and became so popular that Home Missions appointed Myung Suk Lee as its first-ever Korean director of Coffee Break Ministries. Materials that had been used in English-speaking settings since the early 1970s were translated into Korean and used to train new leaders and to attract new members to the Korean congregations that sponsored Coffee Break programs. Lee was not the only leader appointed to work specifically among Korean congregations; soon John Choi was appointed by Home Missions as full-time director of Korean ministries throughout the denomination.

This otherwise upbeat chapter in the story of the CRC did have some unhappy moments in the 1990s. As the denomination moved closer to the full inclusion of women to ordained ministry, a few of the more socially conservative Korean congregations in California began to signal their dismay. By the mid-1990s, when all of the offices of the church were opened to women, the denomination had lost a number of its largest Korean congregations, including the flagship congregation that had been founded by John E. Kim. Kim's church with 1,500 members separated itself from the CRCNA in 1993 and formed the Korean Presbyterian denomination on its own. Not long after, an additional five Korean congregations left the CRC to become part of this new denomination. Nonetheless, the Korean presence in the CRCNA remains vigorous.

But the Korean church is not the only part of the denomination that reflects an increasing ethnic diversity. Los Angeles, California, is one of the most ethnically diverse places anywhere in the world. The Roman Catholic Church celebrates Mass in L.A. each week in over sixty different languages among over one hundred distinct ethnic groups. In this same region the CRCNA includes not only Korean and Hispanic congregations but also Chinese, Vietnamese, Filipino, and Cambodian congregations.

As the CRCNA became more ethnically diverse—and as it continued to reach out to urban populations that were also increasingly populated by ethnic minorities—the denomination had to wrestle with the sensitive subject of racism. Synod 1971 formally authorized the formation of a new denominational agency: the Synodical Committee on Race Relations, also known as SCORR. This new agency was mandated to "design, organize, and implement programs through which the denomination, individual churches, and members can effectively use all available resources to eradicate racism, both causes and effects, within the body of believers and throughout the world."

The timing of SCORR's founding correlated closely with the significant racial strife of that era. Especially in the United States, the period of the late 1960s proved distressing and disorienting. Race riots erupted in Los Angeles, Detroit, and Chicago, even as bus boycotts and freedom rides in the Deep South resulted in atrocious violence against persons of color. The year 1968 was a watershed moment in American history. Following the assassinations of Martin Luther King, Jr., and Robert F. Kennedy, the Democratic National Convention held in Chicago that summer provided the entire nation with yet another arresting spectacle of anger, hatred, and even savagery as whites and blacks clashed outside the convention hall.

Just a few weeks prior to that event, Synod 1968 had passed a resolution calling on the denomination for a day of prayer and racial reconciliation. But the CRC had its own reasons to foster racial understanding and reconciliation. Beginning around 1965, controversy had erupted in Lawndale, Illinois, surrounding the admittance of black children to Timothy Christian School in Cicero, Illinois.

For some years a Christian Reformed congregation had existed in Lawndale on the site of what had once been the CRC's first-ever outreach to Jewish people—the Nathanael Institute. When the Nathanael Institute ministry relocated, the facility was used to reach out to the predominantly African-American population in that area. As the Lawndale church grew, parents of school-age children indicated a desire to send their children to Timothy Christian School in Cicero, which was attended by the area's white children. But despite the fact that Timothy Christian High School in nearby Elmhurst, Illinois, was an integrated school, the school board believed that the Cicero community would not abide the presence of black children. Citing a desire to maintain peace and to protect the safety of all its students, the school board ruled in 1965 to bar black children from attending the school.

The ensuing controversy proved to be wounding for all involved. The issue rose to the level of the synod in the summer of 1968, hence provoking that synod's various declarations on the need for racial reconciliation and understanding within the body of Christ. The Lawndale-Timothy situation lingered for some years, however, and was ultimately resolved less through racial reconciliation and more through the establishment of a Christian school in Lawndale itself.

Despite the acute pain of those years, however, it appears that following these and other similar struggles, the CRCNA emerged with a greater determination to foster racial understanding. Gone were the days when congregations made up of primarily ethnic minority members were referred to as only "associate churches" and when inner-city mission churches were considered "chapels" instead of full-fledged congregations.

By the early 1970s, through the work of SCORR (and later through the ongoing influence of SCORR's successor, the Ministry of Race Relations), the denomination was doing what it could to encourage full participation of ethnic minority persons at all levels of ministry. It also sought to promote racial inclusiveness in the makeup of denominational boards and agencies, at denominationally related colleges and seminaries, and at the annual meeting of synod, which eventually began to invite "ethnic advisors" to attend and address the delegates in the course of their deliberations.

As in all matters of great importance, progress can be slow and comes, as often as not, in fits and starts. But progress was made, principally through the work of Christian Reformed Home Missions and its consistent efforts to establish new congregations made up of ethnic minority worshipers. Still, by the early 1990s the denomination perceived a need to articulate more carefully a biblical and theological vision to guide its ongoing efforts to build a truly multiracial church. At the behest of ideas that emerged from the Multiethnic Conference held that year, Synod 1992 mandated a study committee to articulate "the biblical basis for the development and use of multiethnic leadership" and at the same time to assess how the CRCNA was doing in fostering "a racially and ethnically diverse family of God."

This committee presented Synod 1996 with a comprehensive report that later became known as "God's Diverse and Unified Family." In addition to sketching out a biblical and theological portrait of race and ethnicity, the report challenged synod and the wider denomination to recognize that despite the progress that had been made, there were still "many miles to go" when it came to being a fully unified and inclusive Christian body. Although ethnic diversity had increased over the years in the staffs of denominational agencies and within the ranks of the clergy, many people of color still struggled for full acceptance within the CRCNA, even as they often struggled to achieve a true sense of belonging in their congregations. To help chart a course forward, Synod 1996 adopted the study committee's report, along with all its implications for CRC congregations. In good Reformed fashion, the report fixed one eye on the shalom that existed in God's original good creation while fixing its other eye forward to God's new creation, when people of all races would come together again in God's restored shalom. Synod 1996 again called on congregations to do all in their power to eliminate racism and to enfold as full sisters and brothers in Christ people from all ethnic and racial backgrounds, even as the church lives in anticipation of God's grand reconciling of all things and of all people to himself.

The recommendations were as sweeping as the vision was grand. In the early years of the twenty-first century, few would claim either in the church or in society that the need to overcome racism has ended. Indeed, the 2005 devastation of New Orleans by Hurricane Katrina unleashed a whole new national debate in the United States about race relations and about how it was possible that a permanent underclass defined by race had so clearly developed. Issues surrounding race and ethnicity remain as acute in the twenty-first century as ever, and so Synod 1996's call "to pray and work for reconciliation . . . to continually repent, to strive for justice, and to battle the forces of evil" remains a clarion call and a guiding beacon for the years ahead.

Still, among the things to celebrate and for which to thank God during the sesquicentennial of the CRCNA is the fact that the people attending this particular birthday party come much closer to reflecting the diversity of God's people on earth than at any past point in Christian Reformed history. Along with people who can still trace their roots back to the Netherlands and the earliest ethnic traditions that founded the CRC, the denomination now includes 86 Korean congregations, 26 Hispanic congregations, and 15 Native American congregations. In addition to these congregations, the denomination now includes people from an array of cultures, thus enriching the denomination even as it helps this small portion of the body of Christ to represent God's intricately embroidered tapestry of cultures. Indeed, God's grace extends through every generation and through every tribe, race, and tongue on God's good earth!

ॐ *Chapter Six* ☙

# THE CHANGING FACE OF WORSHIP

I n January 1968 a new show appeared on American television: *Rowan and Martin's Laugh-In*. But *Laugh-In* was more than just a new show—it was a new kind of television altogether. Many Christians objected to the show's suggestive, if not downright bawdy, humor. In any case, there could be no denying that *Laugh-In* broke the mold of most television shows in the twenty years since television had started to become a fixture in ever-increasing numbers of homes.

Among *Laugh-In*'s many innovations was a kind of fast-paced editing style that bombarded the viewer with image after image in rapid-fire fashion. Any given "scene" or skit on the show might last only a few seconds, but in between these already-brief vignettes flashed a barrage of transitional images, each lasting less than a second. Looking back on the show, it's easy to see how this jarring, ever-moving series of images was a forerunner for what would later become the stylistic staple of music videos on cable music networks like MTV and VH1. Gone were the days when Jackie Gleason might present an entire hour-long comedy show using perhaps no more than two fixed cameras. As the television medium matured into the 1970s and 1980s, swiftly changing images from a bevy of vantage points and angles became the norm.

Educators and child psychologists wondered what effect this would have on children and their developmental abilities. Would kids who were used to seeing so much movement and such constantly changing scenery on TV ever be able to concentrate on something as comparatively static as a teacher talking in front of a classroom? Would children raised on fast-paced television dramas and comedies and music videos ever have the patience to sit and read a book?

These questions remain vital even in the early years of the twenty-first century. Whatever the precise effects of TV on the human mind and imagination, there can be little doubt that the availability of such non-stop entertainment has changed people's tastes and expectations. Eventually it also began to affect the church and how it conducts public worship.

But 1968 was not just the year *Laugh-In* began to change the way TV shows were made. It was also the year the Christian Reformed Church— sensing the shifting cultural landscape in North America—did some serious reflecting on the fundamental nature and practice of Christian worship. In the Introduction we noted that in 1957 when the denomination turned 100, liturgical style across the CRC church was, if not uniform exactly, at least exceedingly consistent from east to west and from north to south.

In those days the majority of congregations used number boards at the front of the sanctuary. Each Sunday morning, and again in the evening, members of the congregation would settle into their pews and glance up to the front of the chancel where they would see four or five numbers listed on a board. These numbers represented the *Psalter Hymnal* selections that would be sung during the course of the hour or so of worship. If a person wanted to know which hymn fit where in the service, he or she could flip over the weekly bulletin to see the pre-printed Order of Worship. This order never changed. Indeed, congregations would order enough bulletin covers to last them a year or two. On the front cover would be perhaps a picture of the church, the name of the current pastor, and the times for the two Sunday services. The back cover would have the orders for both the morning and the evening services. The blank pages on the inside were reserved for that week's updates on the sick, notices of upcoming events, and other congregational news. Prior to mid-century, it would have been almost inconceivable to consider using those inside bulletin pages to print up a different order of service every single week!

This was a time in CRC history when pastors paid little attention to liturgical seasons. The same general order of service sufficed for most every Sunday of the entire year. There was no perceived need to have a liturgy unique to Advent or Epiphany or Lent. Certainly there was no

Many congregations still use the number board to list songs from the *Psalter Hymnal*

emphasis on such details as liturgical colors on vestments, stoles, or banners. Litanies or responsive readings were rare, if not unheard of. In many congregations even the Apostles' Creed—although a regular fixture in the standard order of servic—was recited by the pastor alone on behalf of the congregation instead of being recited by all in unison. (As recently as the late 1960s a CRC pastor of my acquaintance was criticized as being too modern when he asked his congregation to recite the Creed along with him!) Baptisms were celebrated as needed, but the celebration of the Lord's Supper was, in most places at least, restricted to four or at most six times per year. Through the mid-twentieth century, Christian Reformed worship was solemn, reverent, and Word-centered . . . but above all it was predictable.

By 2007, however, the situation across the sweep of the CRCNA could hardly be more different. Of course, in many congregations one can still find a liturgical style that is distinctly Reformed and deeply rooted in the traditions that were on singular display at mid-century. But even some of these so-called "traditional services" are frequently spiked with a liturgical sensibility that once did not exist in the denomination. With the advent of *Reformed Worship* magazine in 1986, many pastors and worship leaders began to recover a language and a sensibility about the richness of Christian worship that had, to a large extent, been untapped for many years. Consider that a candidate for the ministry who graduated from Calvin Theological Seminary even as recently as 1990 (when I graduated) is unlikely to have had any instruction in subjects such as the liturgical seasons of the church year, the use of the visual arts in worship, contemporary hymnody, or the construction of worship services for particular moments in the church year. In fact, virtually all of what people of my generation learned about liturgical colors and seasons was something we picked up on our own *after* our seminary education was completed.

The first issue of *Reformed Worship* in 1986

But this interest in the liturgical tradition that the Reformed tradition had left behind or ignored for a while is only a small part of the story. Other cultural and sociological pressures (including the rise of the entertainment culture alluded to earlier) would soon sweep into the church to shake up and, in many places, completely alter the fundamental structure of worship services. But before we get to that part of the story, let's rewind to 1968—to what constitutes another landmark piece of scholarship presented to synod.

## Embracing the Tensions: The 1968 Report

By the early 1960s, recent revolutions in music (particularly the advent of rock-n-roll), the rise of television, and the counter-culture that challenged all things traditional combined to raise some questions about liturgy and worship that had not been asked before. Young people were beginning to learn and to sing new songs that were substantially different in tone and style from the music typically sung in the average Christian Reformed congregation (with not a few such young people deeming traditional hymns and psalms to be staid and boring by comparison).

By 1964 synod had sensed enough ferment in the area of worship that it mandated a study committee "to review all our liturgical literature in the light of its history, its theological content, and the contemporary needs of the churches" and "to study liturgical usages and practices in our churches . . . to advise synod as to the guidance and supervision it ought to provide local congregations in all liturgical matters" (*Agenda* 1968, p. 8). The task was a large one and took the committee four years to fulfill. But in the end, the committee, chaired by John Stek, submitted a substantial and helpful report (whose elegant language was crafted by a man who would go on to become one of the CRCNA's most famous writers, Lewis B. Smedes).

In general, the committee did a remarkable job of embracing the tensions inherent in issues related to Christian worship throughout the ages. Recognizing that worship is always rooted in specific times and places and cultural situations, the committee nowhere tried to develop a one-size-fits-all recommendation. They did summarize and establish certain fundamental dispositions and service elements deemed to be essential to any service of Christian worship, but allowed substantial latitude as to how those essential elements could be incorporated into a given congregation's worship.

Early in its report, the study committee noted that historically a couple of extremes could be observed. On the one side was worship conceived to be flowing in primarily one direction—from us toward God. We as God's people gather and offer to God our praises, confessions, and petitions. On the other side was worship that flowed from the opposite direction—God addresses the people, who receive God's message almost passively. Although admitting that no one tradition ever completely embodied either extreme, the report did single out the Roman Catholic tradition as erring on the side of a passive audience that witnessed the priest's offerings toward God, whereas our own Protestant and Reformed tradition may have erred on the side of so emphasizing the sermon portion of public worship as to make the liturgical flow primarily from God to us. True worship, the report said, should always be a dialogue as worshipers approach their God through prayer and praise even as God comes to his people in Word and sacrament.

The Reformed tradition, however, had long insisted that all of life is in its own way an extended act of worship. In the faithful carrying out of our various vocations, each of us becomes a minister who worships God every moment of every day and in so doing advances God's kingdom in the world. The 1968 report took note of this broader use of the word "liturgy" (which in its original Greek form encompasses the whole of our lifelong service to God and not just what happens when the community formally gathers for a service) but it also nicely said, "to call life a form of worship reveals something about the religious character of life in Christ as it is experienced and practiced outside the sanctuary. But it does not water down or compromise the unique requirements and character of worship proper within the sanctuary. Worship, in the proper sense, is indeed tied to life, relevant to life, a part of life; it is not an escape from life" (*Agenda* 1968, p. 16). This thoughtful balance is characteristic of the entire 1968 report.

Central to the report's insights were the criteria it established by which to evaluate many different forms of liturgy and worship. The committee isolated four motifs that could guide the assessment of any liturgy: biblical, catholic, confessional, and pastoral. In fleshing out these motifs, the study committee once again embraced the tensions inherent in creating worship that is both rooted in the traditions of old and relevant for a given time and place.

Briefly, the biblical motif quite obviously points us to the final arbiter for all of the church's theology, including the content of songs, prayers, sermons, litanies, and creeds. Although the Bible nowhere prescribes a set order of worship, its overall message is properly the final arbiter of all liturgical practice.

The catholic motif provides a fine corrective to any tendency to allow current sociological preferences to so shape the liturgy as to render that liturgy all but unrecognizable to Christians from past ages. For Christian worship truly to be worship, it needs significant theological continuity with the past. "Respect for tradition in liturgy is a fence against individualism and sectarianism. It keeps us from trying to improve the liturgy through gimmickry or novelty for the sake of novelty. It will keep reminding us of what is essential and what is peripheral" (*Agenda* 1968, p. 30).

The confessional motif as developed by the committee notes that a given denomination's practice of worship will quite naturally reflect that denomination's theological approach to Scripture. If the catholic motif roots worship to the tradition and to the ages that have come before, the confessional emphasis brings that tradition to bear on a particular group of people whose interpretation of Scripture may, for instance, include the practice of infant baptism (as opposed to those bodies that read the Bible as insisting on believer-only/adult baptisms).

Finally, the pastoral motif takes careful note of the needs and concerns of a given congregation. "It will always be in tension with the other motifs. For this reason one asks what people are here and now, what their spiritual state and competence is, what their culture is, and what their specific needs are. This is the motif that is born of love, as the others are of faith" (*Agenda* 1968, p. 31).

Within the broad parameters of these guidelines, the report allowed for a good deal of variation. It went on to suggest central elements that ought to be present in every service and provided some sample orders of worship and sample liturgies for the celebration of the Lord's Supper. In and through all of that, the Reformed tradition's emphasis on the preaching of the Word remained central. Although having noted earlier in the report that too much emphasis on the sermon can blunt the dialogic nature of worship, nevertheless there could be no doubting that the place of the Word preached remained front and center in all true worship: "The sermon is the core of the Christian liturgy" (*Agenda* 1968, p. 49).

The report then went on to state some intriguing perceptions on the preaching event. "The liturgy should not catch people by surprise; but preaching must. Liturgy should not keep people tense, nervous, or wary of what comes next. Preaching should keep them tense" (pp. 49-50). But despite this arresting view of the sermon's role in the service, the committee did note that in too many Reformed congregations, that sermon tends also to be the climax of the service. Instead it should always be the living, sacramental encounter with Christ at the Holy Supper that provides the true climax of all worship. Given the frequency with which communion was celebrated in most churches at that time, however, establishing the sacrament as a liturgical climax could not be accomplished without also recommending that churches consider celebrating communion far more often than had been traditionally the case in the CRC. Perhaps partly because of this emphasis, most CRC congregations would in coming years begin to celebrate the Lord's Supper far more often than the four times per year that had long been the norm.

In general, however, how much influence this outstanding report had is an open question. Nearly thirty years later, the denomination revisited the entire matter of worship through a study committee that reported to Synod 1997. This new committee noted that the 1968 report, despite its stellar qualities, had not been "as widely utilized as it deserves to be" (*Worship in a Changing Culture*, p. 6). The 1997 report used the earlier study committee's work as a continuing source of useful instruction and guidance. But by the mid- to late-1990s, there could be no denying that the liturgical landscape had changed dramatically. The very winds of change that the synod had sensed were beginning to flutter already in 1964 grew in intensity in the years immediately after 1968, at times coming to almost gale-force strength in certain communities and congregations.

## Liturgy's New Face

Throughout the twenty years from 1980 to 2000, multiple cultural and ecclesi-astical movements converged in what could be called a liturgical "perfect storm" that swept through congregations of widely different denominations, producing a profusion of liturgical innovation, change, and no small amount of conflict. By the 1990s a new term was being bandied about in church circles: "worship wars." Although proximately centered on music and musical tastes, the deeper, ultimate causes of these wars tied in with distinct movements on the larger church scene in North America and throughout the world.

In 1987 the CRC released its newly revised *Psalter Hymnal*. The ten-year proj-ect was led by Emily Brink (who had also been instrumental in the 1986 found-ing of *Reformed Worship*—indeed, Brink edited the journal for twenty years, retiring from the post in 2006). But Brink's hymnal revision committee was also a kind of CRC *Who's Who?* of musical and liturgical talent. Committee members included church organists Shirley Boomsma and John Hamersma, musicians and composers Dale Grotenhuis, Dale Topp, Jack Van Laar, Marie Post, and Bert Polman, as well as pastors and theologians Anthony Hoekema, Jack Reiffer, and Calvin Seerveld. Their task was not an easy one and, as with all things related to church music, neither would the fruit of the committee's labor be uni-versally appreciated. The new edition (soon dubbed "the gray hymnal") was the first in nearly thirty years, replacing the 1959 edition ("the blue hymnal"). True to its name, the 1987 book contained a mix of both psalms and hymns, but this time included also eighty-six Bible songs (many of contemporary vintage) as well as a few contemporary choruses that had become popular in many churches since the 1960s.

The new *Psalter Hymnal* quickly became the primary songbook in many CRC congregations throughout Canada and the United States. Despite some common laments and complaints ("This gray book is too heavy to hold!" "Why did they change the tune of 'What a Friend We Have in Jesus'?" "Why did they drop my favorite hymn, 'Nearer, Still Nearer'?"), the new hymnal succeeded in providing what many congregations were longing for by the late 1980s and early 1990s: a fresh infusion of at least some of the "new music" that was sweeping through churches everywhere. But even as the new hymnal was finding its way into pew racks throughout the denomination, ecclesiastical and liturgical tectonic plates in North America were

Emily Brink, Editor of the 1987 *Psalter Hymnal*

grinding past each other, causing any number of tremors throughout the wider church.

Liturgical scholar John D. Witvliet believes that three distinct yet ultimately yoked movements converged to generate tremendous energy for liturgical innovation and change by 1990. The first such influence was the explosion of the charismatic and Neo-Pentecostal movement throughout the 1970s and 1980s. As noted earlier in chapter 3, in 1973 the CRCNA officially took notice of the Neo-Pentecostal phenomenon through a well-researched study committee report. But the precise theology of this wing of the charismatic movement notwithstanding, their exuberant style of worship began attracting people in large numbers. Worship in the average Assemblies of God congregation provided a striking—if not startling—contrast to what happened most weeks in the average Christian Reformed congregation. Often led by praise bands or full-blown orchestras, the music and singing in Neo-Pentecostal churches were consistently upbeat, even as the songs themselves were brief, memorable, and usually directly biblical in their lyrics. Members of more traditional denominations like the CRCNA would visit such charismatic churches and find themselves engulfed and powerfully blessed by repeated choruses of songs like "Our God Reigns" and "You Are Worthy." Upon returning to their own congregations, many began to complain about the comparative lack of conviction, enthusiasm, and palpable joy.

A second influence unique to the North American scene is the phenomenon often called "front door evangelism." For Christian Reformed people, especially in the Midwest, this new movement hit home in a powerful way through the innovative work of one of its own covenant children—Bill Hybels. Hybels grew up in the heart of the West Michigan Christian Reformed community but became disenchanted with what he perceived to

be the CRCNA's lack of vitality and active outreach to the lost. In the mid-1970s Hybels began a new kind of church that utilized upbeat music, praise teams, drama, and a small bevy of other innovations that were decidedly "unchurch-like" as a way to draw in Baby Boomers who had become disenchanted by the institutional church but who were nonetheless spiritually hungry. Meeting in an Illinois movie theater, Willow Creek's first service attracted only 125 people. But that would soon change dramatically. Hybel's innovative worship style and non-preachy biblical instruction began to draw ever-larger crowds of "seekers."

Bill Hybels, founder of Willow Creek Church

Within three years the church was attended by 2,000 people every week. By 1981 the church was meeting in a new theater-like auditorium on a 90-acre site in South Barrington, Illinois. By the mid-1990s upwards of 15,000 people were attending some or all of Willow Creek's Sunday and midweek services.

Consistent with the adage "Nothing succeeds in America like success," the idea that worship was itself the front door of evangelistic efforts to reach out to seekers soon caught on. Churches everywhere wanted to become "seeker sensitive" by using what had became known as "the Willow Creek model." Worship that was understandable to only the already-initiated (but difficult to follow for those coming in from the outside) was declared wrong. Instead, every element of the liturgy was scrutinized to see if it was off-putting to those unfamiliar with Christian jargon. In the minds of many, "the Willow Creek model" meant vetting traditional services of everything that could seem strange or unfamiliar to seekers, replacing those elements with easier-to-understand songs, words, and phrases that would reach out to the uninitiated. If worship was to become an evangelism tool, it would need to be reforged.

Despite Willow Creek's own efforts to tell people that their work could not easily be duplicated in established congregations, many churches and church leaders began innovating significant liturgical changes all in the name of reaching out to the "unchurched." In some places, traditional liturgies were shelved in favor of services that some derided as having a kind of "nightclub" format, with fast-paced singing, well-staged dramas, and an ever-shifting change of focus designed to catch the attention of people who had been raised on television and music videos and their ability to entertain through rapid-fire imagery, sound, and music. Others claimed that in some cases so much of the tradition and long history of Christian worship had been changed as to make it appear that the entire church had been in existence for only about five years rather than for nearly 2,000 years.

Recognizing the potential for conflict in such dramatic changes in liturgical style, some congregations attempted to split the difference by keeping a traditional service for those who preferred it and establishing a second contemporary or seeker service for the community and those members of the congregation who wanted worship that was more energetic and upbeat than the traditional service. Still others began to move toward what became known as "blended worship" that combined elements of both the old and the new, the traditional and the contemporary. In any event, there can be little doubting the influence of "front door evangelism" in describing the liturgical shifts that occurred in the latter half of the twentieth century.

But if the charismatic and front door evangelism movements had the effect of jazzing up and re-energizing more traditional forms of worship, a third factor in recent liturgical changes moved in a slightly different direction. Worldwide, beginning already in the 1950s, many church communions began to seek a recovery of past liturgical practices that had been lost or ignored for centuries. The worldwide ecumenical movement went all the way back to the earliest of Christian practices in an effort to restore greater lay participation in public worship, to foster greater unity between the preached Word and the exercise of the sacraments (particularly the Lord's Supper), and to return to ancient rhythms of the church year (including the use of the *Revised Common Lectionary* as a preaching guide). As earlier noted, the CRC also began to tap into the riches and resources of the past, as evidenced

through *Reformed Worship* and its efforts to reestablish liturgical patterns and practices that had long lain fallow. Through this and other in-house resources—and as a result of the worldwide ecumenical liturgical movement—even congregations that did not opt to transform their worship services in the direction of more contemporary or seeker-sensitive avenues nevertheless encountered a wealth of other ideas and possibilities, the adoption of which changed even traditional services.

Because the denomination never mandated a set of rubrics or liturgical templates that all congregations were required to follow (remember that even the 1968 report had resisted foisting any preset liturgies onto the churches), congregations throughout North America were free to experiment and innovate as a result of this confluence of liturgical movements and changes. As a result, in 2007 it is difficult to speak of a "typical" Christian Reformed worship service. In some congregations, worship is strikingly reminiscent of the worship that characterized most all congregations at mid-century. But even in these more traditional services, visitors are likely to find attention paid to the seasons of the church year: they may witness the use of an Advent wreath during December and see liturgical colors used in vestments, clergy stoles, and church banners. Thus "traditional" though these services may be, they nevertheless include elements that many Christian Reformed folk would have found completely foreign to their experience a scant fifty years ago.

These days within the broader CRCNA, worship styles vary widely. Some congregations offer worship that includes a blend of old with new; others, perhaps new church plants, closely resemble a coffeehouse—members sit around tables sipping cappuccino during the service as the pastor, perched on a stool, preaches the Word of God, his message illustrated and buttressed by dramatic skits performed by members of the congregation. Some congregations still use majestic pipe organs to lead the congregation in singing hymns, psalms, and songs; others have long since switched to electric guitars, drum sets, and brass to lead the singing of hymns and songs whose lyrics are projected on screens in front of the chancel. Those screens may be used to show movie clips to illustrate the pastor's sermon or to display visual images that illustrate the theme.

In 1999 the denomination conducted a massive survey of worship practices throughout the CRCNA. The results were telling. According to an executive summary of the survey prepared by Gayla R. Postma, 60 percent of Christian Reformed congregations had moved in the direction of more blended forms of worship, even as most of the other congregations reported having made at least some substantial alterations to their form of worship on Sundays. Although a strong 89 percent of CRC churches used the 1987 edition of the *Psalter Hymnal,* over a third used another songbook in addition to the denominational mainstay, even as 70 percent projected song lyrics onto screens at least some of the time. The survey also showed that whereas traditional church choirs seemed to be declining in number, "praise teams" of people who helped lead the congregation in singing more contemporary songs were on the rise. Overall, by the turn of the twenty-first century, the CRCNA remained a mix of the old with the new. But the rise of these newer forms of worship was the big story over the past quarter-century of the denomination's history.

What the future holds for worship in the Christian Reformed Church (or anywhere) is by no means clear. Somewhat to the surprise of the Baby Boomer generation (which was the force behind the seeker-sensitive movement in innovating a thoroughly contemporary form of worship completely unlike what had been practiced by previous generations), in the early twenty-first century many young people in Generations X and Y began to express a yearning to return to the mysteries of ancient forms of worship, with not a few such college-age people turning to the Eastern and Greek Orthodox traditions and their richly embroidered form of ancient liturgical patterns. In the early years of the twenty-first century, yet another new term was being used to describe youth patterns in worship: the "emerging church" movement that restored many of the same liturgical practices and rituals that the seeker-sensitive movement had dismantled as too "churchy" in the 1980s. What seems certain to be true for the foreseeable future is that interest in all things liturgical will continue to grow.

One sign of this interest is the overwhelming success in the last ten years of the Calvin Institute for Christian Worship and particularly its annual Worship Symposium in January. Symposium was started as a very small event spearheaded by John D. Witvliet and some like-minded college and graduate school friends. Soon, however, the annual gathering swelled to 500, then 750, then 1,000, and then 1,500 people who traveled to Grand Rapids, Michigan, in the dead of winter for three days of stimulating conversation on a vast array of worship-related topics, from the use of the fine arts to music for children, from intelligent utilization of drama in worship to effective use of technology. If Symposium alone is any indication, people in churches everywhere are more committed than ever to fostering worship that glorifies God and edifies God's people, and so equips the entire church for mission to a world in need of hearing God's good news.

# LOOKING AHEAD TO GENERATIONS TO COME

**W**hen my former teacher and friend David Engelhard asked me to write this book in January 2004, he reminded me that although first and foremost a history of the denomination, the book's conclusion would need to look ahead. Perched, as we are, in the early years of the twenty-first century, what does the balance of this century hold for the Christian Reformed Church? What might the author of the bicentennial volume on Christian Reformed history write about in 2057?

Life changes fast. In fact, cultural, social, and technological advances and leaps seem to occur at a far swifter pace in recent years than in all of the history that led up to this present moment. What other single century in human history witnessed advances and change on a par with the twentieth century? My great-grandmother Elizabeth Hoezee lived to be nearly 100 years old and died in the late twentieth century. When she was born, horses were the sole source of local transportation (and even locomotive trains were still a novelty). By the time she died, space shuttles were routinely rocketing into orbit. Who would have predicted such meteoric leaps at the beginning of the twentieth century when my great-grandmother was a young girl?

Looking into the future is at best a perilous enterprise; we don't know what lies ahead. What makes prognostications about the church even more difficult is that the entire subject of the future of denominations has been a source of great controversy for some time now. Savvy church historians like Martin E. Marty have predicted the demise of denominations. Among the reasons for this prediction is the fact that in recent years people of faith have found more ties of commonality horizontally, *across* denominational lines, than they have vertically or *within* their own communions. That is, an evangelically minded Presbyterian may well find more in common with certain Roman Catholics and Methodists than with many other fellow Presbyterians.

Billy Graham presents a book to Pope John Paul II during an audience on Jan. 12, 1981, at the Vatican.

Or consider another example: many in the CRCNA today can still remember days when parents or grandparents spoke rather disdainfully about Roman Catholics. Yet in the late twentieth century many evangelicals and Christian Reformed people spoke glowingly about Pope John Paul II and deeply mourned his death in 2005. People of many faiths made common cause with John Paul not because the theology of the Catholic Church had tilted decisively in the direction of more Reformed and Protestant sensibilities but because of his strong stands on social issues like abortion, euthanasia, and gay marriage.

In addition to this trans-denominational seeking after unity and commonality, the past quarter-century has also witnessed an overall loosening of loyalty to denominations. People wear their denominational labels lightly now. In the 1980s and 90s it was widely believed that seekers from the Baby Boomer generation were turned off by denominations. Just seeing "Christian Reformed

Church" or "Methodist" or "Presbyterian" on a church sign was enough to turn off social dissidents from the 1960s (who once defined themselves by the slogan "Question Authority"). Denominations smacked of institutionalized religion, of restrictive structures and rules and creedal statements that tended to stifle a living, vibrant faith.

Hence, even many congregations that were part of the CRCNA opted for church names that rendered their denominational affiliation invisible. Such congregations were not, in so doing, distancing them-

Denominational affiliation is not always evident on church signs.

selves from the denomination, its beliefs, or its governing structures. Indeed, much of the growth in new members that the denomination has experienced in the last thirty years has come precisely through new church plants, many of whose formal names do not include the words "Christian Reformed Church," but who eventually introduce people to the Christian Reformed tradition in new and fresh ways.

Still, there can be little doubt that this loosening of overt ties to denominational bodies reflects a larger sociological pattern that leads away from what once defined and unified people of faith (namely, their distinctive denominational stripes). The fact that the largest mega churches in the United States are almost all nondenominational likewise may be a predictor of the future. Styles of worship, stances on key socio-political issues, and sometimes affinity with and loyalty to a single charismatic preacher are now far more important to many people than being part of a denomination that is defined by its common history, its ethnic origins, or its confessional documents. One major advantage that denominations traditionally had was the ability to pool resources so as to do greater works collectively than any one congregation could do by itself. But since Lakewood Church in Houston, Texas, now counts 16,000 people as members, the idea that you need to be part of a larger denomination no longer sounds very credible. Some churches are large enough to do great collective work all on their own.

Overarching these church-specific discussions, however, is the unhappy fact that the earliest years of the twenty-first century have proven to be very divisive. The twenty-first century in the United States got off to a bang late in 2000 with the most disputed, controversial, and flat-out closest presidential election in over a century. Less than a year later, however, the terrible events of 9/11 seemed for a brief while to be a unifying moment, both for citizens of the United States but also in solidarity with people from many nations. People in the heartland wore T-shirts bearing the words "We're All New Yorkers Now," even as a newspaper in France declared, "Today We Are All Americans." But the unity did not last. By 2004 another deeply divisive presidential election took place in the shadow of a war that likewise was pitting family members against one another. Within the span of only a few short years, suddenly Americans defined their own country in the previously unheard-of terms of "red states" and "blue states."

Such fractious times in the larger world tends to infect churches also. By the beginning of 2006 when this book was being completed, several of the largest denominational bodies in the United States and Canada were teetering on the brink of schism. The immediate cause for most such potential splits were questions surrounding homosexuality, gay marriage, and the ordination of gay priests/pastors. But as vital as such questions are, those specific subjects were part and parcel of an entire tangle of related issues. Often bound up with a person's stance on any given social issue are a welter of related political and social subjects, including his or her view of Scripture. In some cases, preachers began to note that even certain innocent phrases used in sermons were being seized on by some in the congregation as indicative of a potentially divisive viewpoint or agenda that the preacher was allegedly promoting in a partisan way.

Tense times such as those that exist in these early years of the twenty-first century sometimes abate almost as quickly as they began. It is difficult to know whether current trends toward fragmentation will continue. But the presence of such tensions, not to mention the glaring fact that the church is being confronted with uncomfortable questions related to homosexuality and other issues, raises questions about the future.

Will the CRCNA still exist in 2057? Will there be a definable denomination left to celebrate its bicentennial? Despite the pressures being faced by all church communions—and despite the fact that future synodical decisions on a number of questions may well cause occasional splinters and splits as they have throughout the past 150 years—it seems more likely than not that the CRCNA will continue to exist in some form. But even as the denomination at 150 looks vastly different than it did when it celebrated its hundredth birthday, so it seems all but certain that the next fifty years will introduce changes in the denomination at least as great, if not greater, than those of the last half-century.

What might some of those changes be? It seems likely that innovation and changes in worship format and style will continue. If the "emerging church" phenomenon is any indication, perhaps some future changes will involve a creative recapturing of past traditions. For instance, after many years when preaching based on the themes in the Heidelberg Catechism was in decline in the CRC, recently some younger church planters have "rediscovered" the Catechism as a potentially valuable ally in introducing the faith to postmodern pilgrims who have a very limited knowledge of Christianity. Similarly, college students in the early years of this new century have begun to express a desire to move past the praise choruses that had been written in more recent years so as to return to singing the grand hymns of the past. Naturally, these features of our collective past are not reintroduced in a vacuum, that is, completely unchanged from their past forms. Rather, the old is blended with the new and woven into the new liturgical tapestry that has been created during these last twenty or so years of liturgical change and reform in ways that provide continuity across centuries of Christian faith and practice. The point is that future liturgies and worship services will no doubt continue to change—sometimes even in dramatic fashion—but part of the change may include some of what was familiar to Christian Reformed people even at mid-century.

One thing that is fairly easy to predict about the future of our denomination is that it will continue to diversify culturally and ethnically in ways that will enrich us all. The world is a smaller place now than it was for past generations. Contact with people from faith traditions and societies vastly different from their own is now a commonplace for young people. Just as the GIs came back from Europe and Asia as changed people after World War II half a century ago, so young people today are being changed by what they see and experience as citizens of a global community through people and societies from widely divergent locations. As individuals and groups from across the spectrum of earth's rainbow of cultures make the CRCNA their adopted faith home, we may all learn new ways to speak of, think about, and practice our faith.

But that same shrinking of the world that brings all of us in touch with rich cultural diversity and traditions has also been a source of global conflict. Particularly after 9/11, many began to speculate that the world could be on the verge of a new kind of world war that would pit East against West, Christianity against Islam, democratic societies against more theocratically controlled cultures. If the twenty-first century becomes more religiously inflamed—if persecution of Christians by Muslims or of Muslims by Christians becomes more common—then this would have an effect on the entire church. Periods of persecution may well cause Christian believers from all walks of life to huddle together more and emphasize what is held in common rather than what differentiates. On the other hand, it seems likely that if this kind of global conflict is avoided, it will be due in no small part to a rise in tolerance and a willingness to embrace the tensions inherent in a global society. If this happens, then even people as deeply committed to the faith and to orthodox formulations of doctrine as those in the CRC traditionally have been may need to learn new ways of interacting with the wider world and new ways to bear witness to the gospel truth in Christ Jesus the Lord.

Beyond such broad possibilities, who can say what may happen? Could the day come when the fracture of 1857 will be healed as the Reformed Church in America and the CRCNA come back together as a single denomination? Certainly there has been a good deal of talk about such a prospect. As Christians everywhere begin to make common cause with like-minded believers from a variety of denominations, the two denominations might well decide that what they have in common more than compensates for the differences that divided them. Might portions of the CRC join with disaffected Presbyterian cousins? This too is a possibility, the realization of which would depend on a hundred large and small events that may still be years from unfolding (if they happen at all).

However this all shakes out, one prediction is both easy to make and certain to be fulfilled: namely, that the CRCNA will be strikingly different at its bicentennial in 2057 than it is now in 2007. But no matter what happens, with

Worshipers at Hope International Church, Arcadia California.

utmost confidence I predict that the CRCNA at 200 (or at 175 or 250 or 300) will still be a place where "grace through every generation" is evident. Someone once commented that the fact that the Christian church still exists in ever-growing numbers nearly two millennia after Jesus rose again from the dead counts as its own kind of miracle. After all, once upon a time, a group of no more than a dozen untutored disciples fell to pieces when faced with the grim reality of their Master's brutal execution upon a Roman cross. Yet a scant two months later the weakest and most knock-kneed of that bunch stood up to declare the crucified One "both Lord and Christ." No sooner had Peter preached the gospel for the first time on Pentecost than people responded, "What shall we do?" Peter told them to repent, to be baptized, and to receive the forgiveness of sins that Christ Jesus the Lord had made possible. "The promise is for you and for your children," Peter said, "and for all who are far off."

It seems highly unlikely that on that grand day Peter could have imagined people as "far off" as we Christian Reformed sisters and brothers some twenty centuries later. Peter would be among the first to confess his surprise that the Lord has tarried this long. But if Peter could chat with us for a little while all this time later, he'd soon hear us Christian Reformed folks in the early twenty-first century confessing Jesus as Lord and naming him as our only comfort in life and in death. And you can only imagine how the old fisherman turned apostle would smile. After all, joy is the proper reaction for all God's children when we see so clearly that God's grace has remained strong and steadfast through every generation.

So I close this book with a smile on my own face as I wish you grace and peace through our Lord Jesus Christ. Grace and peace be unto you, to your children and grandchildren, and to all who are as yet "far off" but who one day will be brought near through the grace of our Lord Jesus Christ, the love of God the Father, and the ongoing fellowship of the Holy Spirit. Amen!

# BIBLIOGRAPHY

*Acts of Synod* 1966; 1967; 1971; 1972; 1973; 1984; 1995. Grand Rapids, Mich.: CRC Publications.

*Agenda for Synod* 1968; 1973; 1978. Grand Rapids, Mich.: CRC Publications.

*Authentic Worship in a Changing Culture.* Grand Rapids, Mich.: Faith Alive Christian Resources, 1997.

Barnes, Craig. *Searching for Home: Spirituality for Restless Souls.* Grand Rapids, Mich.: Brazos, 2003.

Beets, Henry. *The Christian Reformed Church: Its Roots, History, Schools, and Mission Work.* Grand Rapids, Mich.: Baker Book House, 1946.

Bratt, James. *Dutch Calvinism in Modern America: A History of a Conservative Subculture.* Grand Rapids, Mich.: Eerdmans, 1984.

Hoezee, Scott and Christopher Meehan. *Flourishing in the Land.* Grand Rapids, Mich.: Eerdmans, 1996.

Hofman, Tymen E. *The Canadian Story of the CRC: Its First Century.* Ontario: Guardian Books, 2004

Marty, Martin E. *Modern American Religion Volume 1: The Irony of It All: 1893-1919.* Chicago: The University of Chicago Press, 1986.

Schaap, James. *Our Family Album: The Unfinished Story of the Christian Reformed Church.* Grand Rapids, Mich.: CRC Publications, 1998.